Learning

Photoshop CS6

with 100 practical exercises

Learning

Photoshop CS6
with 100 practical exercises

www.mcb-press.com

Learning Photoshop CS6 with 100 practical exercises

Presentation

LEARNING PHOTOSHOP CS6 WITH 100 PRACTICAL EXERCISES

This book provides 100 practical exercises that take you for a tour of the main functions of the program. While it is impossible to collect all the features of Photoshop CS6 in the pages of this book, we have chosen the most interesting and useful ones. Once you have completed the 100 exercises that make up this book, you will be able to use the program and carry out all those retouches that are typically performed with images and photographs, both professionally and personally, with ease.

THE WAY TO LEARN

Our experience in the field of education has lead us to design this manual, where every function is learned by carrying out a practical exercise. The exercises are explained step-by-step and click by click, to avoid confusion in the execution of the process. In addition, the exercises are illustrated with descriptive images of the most important steps or the results that should be obtained, and also with IMPORTANT boxes that provide further information on each of the topics covered in the exercises.

This system ensures that upon completion of the 100 exercises that make up this manual, the user will be able to be able to comfortably use the basic tools of Photoshop CS6 and get the best out of them.

FILES REQUIRED

If you want to use the sample files that appear in this book, they can be downloaded from ~~www.marcombo.com.~~ → (Spanish)

mcb-press.com is English

files not available as of 11/2013

WHO SHOULD READ THIS MANUAL

If you are starting to practice and work with Photoshop, you will find a complete tour of the main functions in these pages. However, if you are an expert in the program, this manual will also be very useful to see more advanced aspects or review specific functions, which you can find in the contents section.

Each exercise is treated independently, so it is not necessary to do them in order (although we recommend it, since we have attempted to group exercises thematically). Thus, if you need to address a specific issue, you will be able to go directly to the exercise where the issue is dealt with and carry it out on your own computer.

PHOTOSHOP CS6

Image editing is an increasingly common task among design enthusiasts and photographers in general, so this latest version of Photoshop, CS6, incorporates new tools and utilities that allow you to cover practically all environments where digital imaging is needed: web design, multimedia, art, illustration, as well as scientific and medical uses, and so on.

Without a doubt, Photoshop is one of the most widely used photo retouching and editing programs and is respected by professionals and trainees of digital image editing. The main uses are discussed in this comprehensive manual.

Photoshop CS6, with many more new and interesting features, lets you take full advantage of the program to achieve spectacular results, high quality and a completely professional appearance.

How **"Learning..."** books work

The title of each exercise concisely expresses what it is about. Thus, if you are interested, you can go directly to the action you want to learn or review.

The exercises have been systematically written step-by-step, so that you will never get lost during their execution.

The number to the right of the page tells you clearly in what exercise you are.

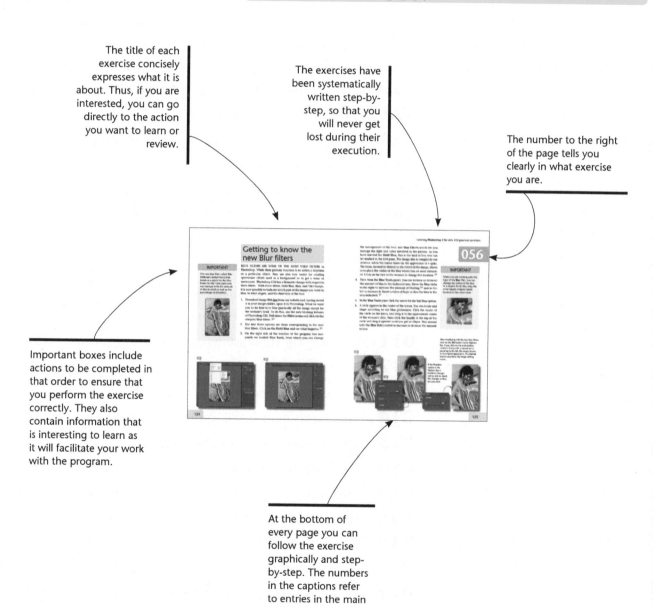

Important boxes include actions to be completed in that order to ensure that you perform the exercise correctly. They also contain information that is interesting to learn as it will facilitate your work with the program.

At the bottom of every page you can follow the exercise graphically and step-by-step. The numbers in the captions refer to entries in the main text.

Table of contents

Table of contents

Getting to know the Photoshop CS6 Interface

PHOTOSHOP CS6 PRESENTS A NEW INTERFACE. The changes are more in relation to color than element arrangement. At the top of the window you can find the menu bar, and just below is the Options Bar, the content of which will depend on the selected tool. Arranged vertically to the left of the screen is the Tools panel. The remaining panels are on the right-hand side and can be hidden or distributed in the work area by modifying panel position and size. New to this version of the program is the Timeline panel, which is shown by default in the bottom panel, and which shares this space with another new addition: the Mini Bridge.

1. In this first exercise we will take a short walk through the Photoshop CS6 interface. If you have an earlier version of Photoshop, when you access the program for the first time, you can migrate the default settings of the previous interface to the new one.

2. Visually Photoshop CS6 is very different since the interface color is much darker than previous versions. 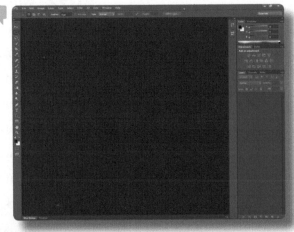 The workspace switcher location, by default in the **Essentials** workspace mode, has changed location and is now above the panel

As shown in this pop-up box you can migrate adjustments among different versions, by clicking the **Migrate Presets** option of the **Presets** command, which is in the **Edit** menu of the application.

From the program's preferences box it's possible to recover the interface color of previous versions.

1

Migrate Presets From Previous Versions of Adobe Photoshop

Would you like to migrate presets from the following versions?
Adobe Photoshop CS5.1

Yes   No

2

area on the far right of the Options Bar. Display this field to see the available options.

3. As you see, it is possible to maintain basic workspace view mode with the new features. In addition, depending on the type of work you are doing, you will be able to choose among different workspace modes. Note that the same options are available in the **Workspace** command from the **Window** menu. Keep the **Essential** mode selected by clicking it.

4. On the right-hand side of the workspace you will see three groups of panels displayed by default. The first group contains two tabs, **Color** and **Swatches**. From this panel you can assign different types of fillers and swatches. To collapse these panels, click the double arrow that appears at the right end of the title bar.

5. The second group of panels, **Adjustments,** and **Styles,** contains styles and adjustments commands. Click the double arrow button as before to return to the expanded mode.

6. The third set of panels, **Layers**, **Channels**, and **Paths**, is for managing exactly that: layers, channels, and paths. At the bottom of the window, grouped under one panel are the **Mini Bridge** group panel, previously accessible from the vertical panel bar, and the **Timeline** panel.

IMPORTANT

To the left of the panel zone you can see two small icons: the first opens the History panel and the second, which is new to this version, the **Properties** panel.

Access to the Mini Bridge was previously in the same place as the **History** panel.

Managing the interface panels

IT IS POSSIBLE TO INCREASE YOUR SCREEN SPACE to the maximum while maintaining access to the most common tools if the panels are conveniently organized. Tool panels become independent floating panels that can be dragged and manually distributed in the workspace area. Active panels are highlighted in the Window menu. Click the Tab key to hide all panels at once.

1. In this exercise you will learn to manipulate Photoshop panels according to your work requirements. You will begin by partially concealing one of the default groups. Double-click the **Color** panel tab. **1**

2. Except for the tabs that remain visible, the information contained in the corresponding group is automatically hidden. **2** This space saver feature is especially useful when too many panels are opened and extra workspace is temporarily needed. Click the **Color** panel tab.

3. The panels are not fixed elements and can be distributed across the workspace area. Click the **Layers** panel tab, **3** and

The key combination **Shift + Tab** hides all panels except the Tools panel and Options Bar.

with the mouse button pressed drag it to the center of the workspace.

4. The panel is now a floating bar with its own option menu and exit command button. To return it to its original position, drag it back to that point. (You will see a pop-up blue frame indicating the panel group it will be anchored to when you release the mouse button.)

5. Keep in mind that by dragging the corresponding panel tab you can change the order in which panels are displayed within their groups. For example, click the **Color** panel tab and drag it to place it to the right of the **Swatches** panel.

6. Finally, to close the panel group, click the **Options** button and press **Close Tab Group**.

7. You can reopen any of these panels or panel groups by using the **Window** menu. It provides access to all of the application panels, so go ahead and click **Color**.

8. Follow the same procedure to hide the **Timeline** panel group, at the bottom of the interface, in this version opened by default, or use the context menu. To finish this exercise, right-click the **Mini Bridge** panel tab and select the **Close Tab Group** tab in the drop-down menu.

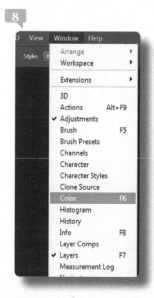

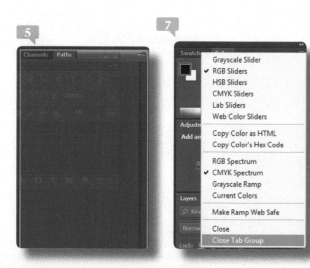

In this new version of the program, new options have been added to the options menu in the **Color** panel and the **Samples** panel.

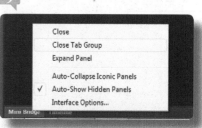

Browsing files in the Bridge and Mini Bridge

IMPORTANT

The Mini Bridge allows you to open your images in Photoshop with a simple double-click. If however you choose the drag technique instead, keep in mind that the image content will be placed on top of the existing image.

ADOBE BRIDGE IS A FILE BROWSER to view, sort, or edit files. Files are organized before displaying them on screen: creating, duplicating, deleting, and moving new folders and files. Although not a new addition in itself, Photoshop CS6 has moved the Mini Bridge to a new location: at the bottom of the interface sharing space with the Timeline panel. With Mini Bridge you can create thumbnails, update files, and work with them in a much more simple way.

1. In order to use Mini Bridge you need to have Bridge opened and running in the background. You can do this either by clicking **Browse in Bridge** in the **File** menu, or go to the **Mini Bridge** panel. Pull down the **File** menu and click on the **Browse in Mini Bridge** command.

2. The **Mini Bridge** opens and tells you to run Bridge simultaneously. Use the command **Launch Bridge** to run the main file browser.

3. By default, the Mini Bridge uploads the Desktop content. On the left-hand side is a list of available disk drives on your computer. On the upper part of the panel is a command bar to

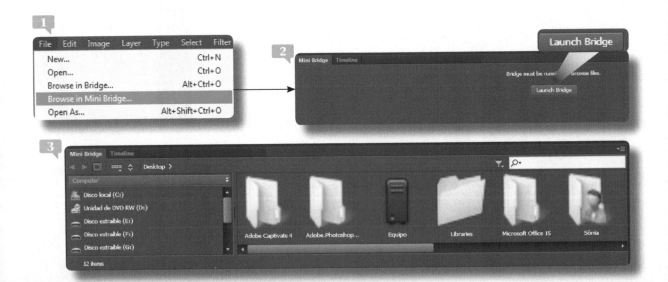

navigate the folder system visualized in the center of the panel, view content in Bridge, edit files in different modes, and change the way they are organized in the images folder on your computer as well as access content by double-clicking.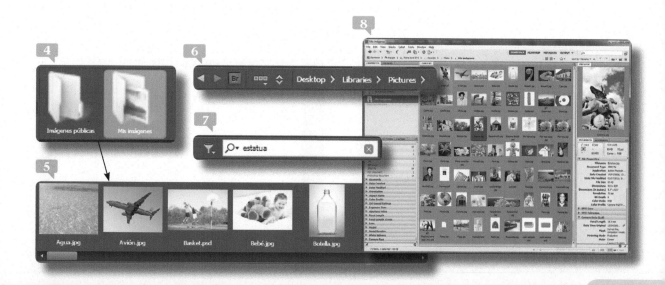

4. The images contained in the folder are now in thumbnail mode. Use the command bar to view the corresponding folder and directory. Use the horizontal scroll bar to view the remaining images.

5. The images are ordered alphabetically. On the right-hand side of the command bar there is an icon that lets you apply filters to your images and a search field from where you can locate specific files in the opened folder. In Mini Bridge you can open the images in Bridge and Photoshop. In the first instance, select the image you want and click the third icon in the command bar.

6. The Bridge interface is divided into three parts. To the left is the folder panel and the filters, collections and exports panel; the central part displays the image catalog; and on the right-hand side you will find the preview panes and property panels of images. To finish this exercise, open the **File** menu and click on the command **Return to Adobe Photoshop** to return to Photoshop.

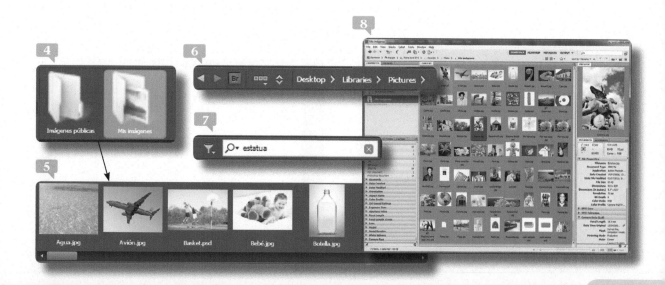

Customizing the work area

CUSTOMIZING THE WORK AREA OF PHOTOSHOP is a new feature of CS6, it allows you to reuse the interface color from a previous version. In addition, Photoshop allows you to reconfigure the tools available in the work area and keep a specific selection of them.

1. In this exercise will learn how to customize the workspace and save those settings to have it available at any time. Begin by accessing the **Preferences** dialog box, where you can change the look of the interface. You will see that the interface is much darker than in previous versions of Photoshop. Pull down the **Edit** menu, click **Preferences**, and select **Interface** from the drop-down list.

2. The preferences dialog box appears, which shows the contents of the **Interface** category. Go to the Appearance section to make changes. As you can see, there is an even darker tone and two lighter ones. Try the color of previous versions of the interface according to your preferences. Keep in mind that these changes will be applied when the application is restarted.

3. Here, you can see the change in the program interface, and it shows you how to save and retrieve a workspace. Click the Options button in the **Color** panel and select **Close Tab Group**.

4. To display the icons in the **Tools** panel in two columns. Click on the double arrow that appears at the side.

5. To save this workspace, click the **Window** menu, click on the **Workspace** option, and select **New Workspace**.

6. In the **New Workspace** dialog box, you must name the current workspace to save it. Type, for example, the term **No color** in the **Name** field.

7. Once you have assigned a name, you can indicate if you want the program to remember the layout of the keyboard shortcuts and menus. The panel locations are automatically stored with the new workspace. Select the two options of the section **Capture** and click the **Save** button.

8. The program will have saved the current configuration of the workspace, as seen in the workspace selector. We will now see how to eliminate it. You should know that you can delete any workspace that isn't active. Change the current workspace to the default **Essential**, display the spaces selector, and click on the **Delete Workspace** command.

9. In the dialog box of the same name, you must choose the layout you want to delete. This time, keep the name **No color**, press the **Delete** button, and then click on the **Yes** button in the confirmation box.

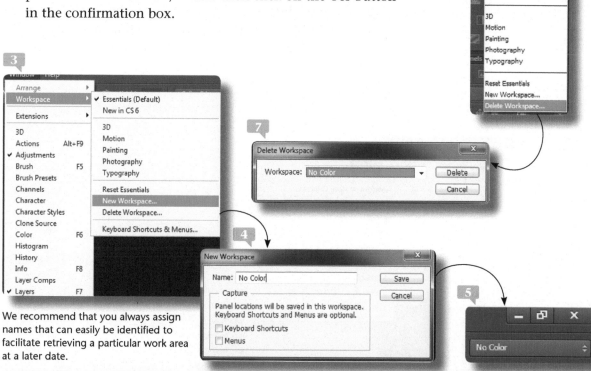

We recommend that you always assign names that can easily be identified to facilitate retrieving a particular work area at a later date.

Customizing the application menus

IMPORTANT

When working with the setup of the keyboard shortcuts and menus, notice that at the top of your workspace the field **Set** indicates that the default settings of Photoshop have been modified.

Set: Photoshop Defaults (modified)

FOLLOWING THE PERSONALIZATION of the work environment, Photoshop allows you to adapt each of the program's menus to your tastes and needs. Since the option keyboard shortcuts and menus are contained in the workspace command from the Window menu, the user can access a dialog box to perform this procedure.

1. Open the **Window** menu, click on the **Workspace** command and choose **Keyboard Shortcuts & Menus**.

2. The **Keyboard Shortcuts & Menus** box opens showing the contents of the **Menus** tab. The information contained on this page refers to the original layout of Photoshop and the menu commands. The middle box lists the menus, where you can find their commands. Click on the arrow preceding the name on the **File** menu.

3. The menus are displayed in this list in the order they were presented in the program. Next to each command is the image of an eye in the **Visibility** column. Clicking on this image allows you to show or hide commands in each menu. Click on the corresponding menu command **Open As**.

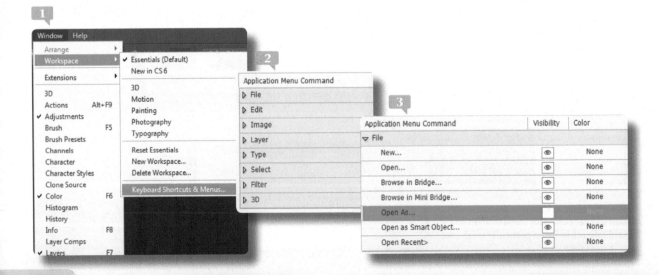

4. From now on this command from the **File** menu will not be displayed. Another of the interesting possibilities for personalizing the menus is one which allows different colors to be used to highlight the options that you use most often. Click on the arrow preceding the **File** menu to hide its contents and click on the **Edit** menu.

5. To the right of the column **Visibility**, the **Color** column is shown. Click on the word **None** in the **Color** column for the command **Step Forward** and, in the small palette of colors that appears, click on the color **Orange**.

6. Before finishing you will save this modification but for now, let's see what other aspects can be configured from this menu. Press the arrow for the **Menu** field.

7. This box contains the option, **Panel Menus**, that will allow you to make the same modifications that we saw for menu commands, but on the options contained in the panels. Click on the first of the icons to the right of the field **Set**.

8. This opens the **Save** dialog box, displaying the contents of the Photoshop **Customize Menu** folder where all workspace configurations relating to the menus are stored. Type the word **Menus** in the **Name** field and click the **Save** button.

9. Click the OK button in the program and see the option Open Recent is not shown on the **File** menu, and the option **Step Forward** in the **Edit** menu is highlighted with the chosen color.

Creating and modifying keyboard shortcuts

KEYBOARD SHORTCUTS ARE KEY COMBINATIONS that allow you to perform actions that would normally be performed from a menu item. Keyboard shortcuts are a direct way to work and can be managed from the Keyboard Shortcuts tab in the Keyboard Shortcuts and Menus box.

1. Access the box **Keyboard Shortcuts & Menus** using the **Keyboard Shortcuts** option in the **Edit** menu.

2. First, click the **Create a new set based on the current set of shortcuts**, the second to the right of the field **Set**.

3. This opens the **Save** box showing the default folder **Photoshop Keyboard Shortcuts**, where you will store a copy of the default values. (This file has a .KYS extention.) Press the **Save** button.

4. The program displays default keyboard shortcuts, which often coincide with those of most applications. For example, to create a new blank document, use **Ctrl + N** or to copy items press **Ctrl + C**. From this tab you can change these combinations if one of them seems difficult or impossible to remem-

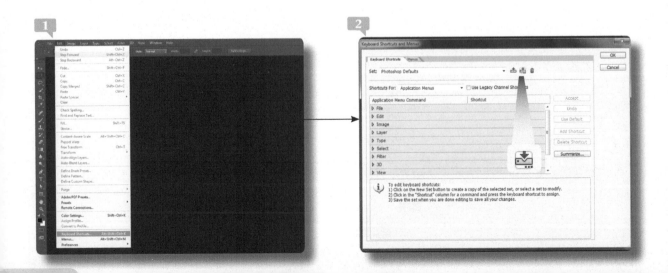

ber. You should note that the same shortcut cannot be used for two different actions. Now look at the menu command you want to assign a keyboard shortcut to. Click on the arrow preceding the **Edit** menu, click on the bottom of the vertical scroll bar and select the **Check Spelling** command.

5. As you can see, this option has no shortcut assigned to it. Let's see what happens if you choose one that already belongs to another action. Press, for example, the **F6** key to be inserted in the text field of the **Shortcut** column.

6. The program tells you that this keyboard shortcut is already assigned to the **Color** function of the **Window** menu. Now try **Alt + F6** and then press **Return**.

7. Photoshop does not give any warning message, so we deduce that the combination is available. You can add new combinations for the same action using the **Add shortcut** button and delete the assigned shortcut using the **Delete shortcut** button. Press that button.

8. As you now see, **Check spelling** does not have any keyboard shortcut assigned to it, so you have to run it from the **Edit** menu. To restore the default settings in Photoshop, click on the icon that shows a trash can.

9. Click the **Yes** button to confirm and then close the dialog box by pressing the **OK** button.

IMPORTANT

You can access the box **Keyboard Shortcuts & Menus** from the Edit menu or from the Workspace submenu of the Window menu. Before you edit the keyboard shortcuts, make a copy of the default workspace using the icon that shows a floppy disk and an arrow.

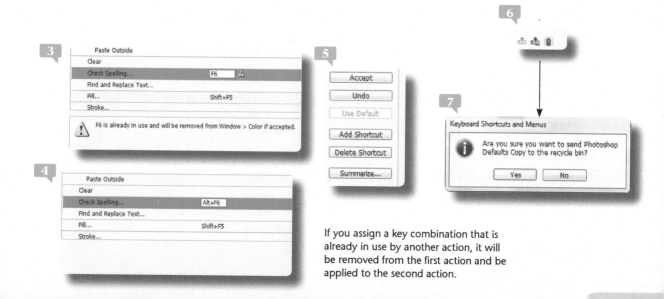

If you assign a key combination that is already in use by another action, it will be removed from the first action and be applied to the second action.

Creating, opening, and saving files

NEW PHOTOSHOP DOCUMENTS, also known as canvases, show measurements. A default background color can be customized by the user. The actions that create new documents and open files are carried out through the menu options file, Adobe Bridge, or by using the familiar keyboard shortcuts. The files created in Photoshop must be saved to be used on later occasions.

1. To create a blank canvas, click the **File** menu and select **New.**

2. The **New** dialog box displays the options you need to specify for the new file, including the dimensions of the new file, the color mode, and the background color. Keep the default options shown and click **OK.**

3. The canvas appears in a window with a tab where you can see the main features of the file: the name of the document, the zoom ratio, and, in parentheses, the default color mode, which is RGB. Since you won't use the new blank document, for the moment press the small x on the file tab to close it.

4. Next, you will access a sample of the images stored on the computer. To load an image and display it in the workspace,

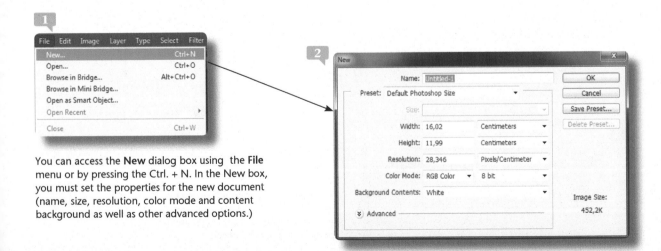

You can access the **New** dialog box using the **File** menu or by pressing the Ctrl. + N. In the New box, you must set the properties for the new document (name, size, resolution, color mode and content background as well as other advanced options.)

use the **Open** command from the **File** menu or press **Ctrl + O**. Clic de **Open** command.

5. In the **Open** box, locate and open the **Sample Images** folder, select an image and click **Open**.

6. The picture has now been opened on a separate canvas, ready to be retouched. 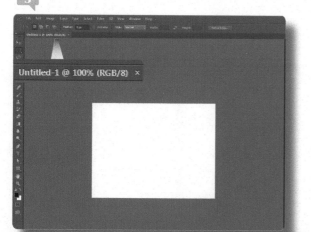 You can now save the image in Photoshop's own format. Open the **File** menu and choose **Save As**.

7. In the **Save As** box, you must choose a name and a format for the image and indicate where you want it to be saved. Open the **Format** field and choose **Photoshop PSD**.

8. Now browse for and select the image library and then press the **Save** button.

9. There is now a copy of the image in PSD, which is currently open. If you make changes to it, use the **Save** command or press **Ctrl + S** regularly so that the changes are stored. Similarly, if you close the image before saving your changes, Photoshop will display a message to prompt you to save the changes before closing. To finish this exercise, close the image by clicking on the x of the tab.

007

IMPORTANT

If you have multiple documents open, you can close them one at a time, clicking on the small x, or you can all at once by using the **Close All** option from the **File** menu.

5

JPEG (*.JPG;*.JPEG;*.JPE)
Photoshop (*.PSD;*.PDD)
Large Document Format (*.PSB)
BMP (*.BMP;*.RLE;*.DIB)
CompuServe GIF (*.GIF)
Dicom (*.DCM;*.DC3;*.DIC)
Photoshop EPS (*.EPS)
Photoshop DCS 1.0 (*.EPS)
Photoshop DCS 2.0 (*.EPS)
IFF Format (*.IFF;*.TDI)
JPEG (*.JPG;*.JPEG;*.JPE)
JPEG 2000 (*.JPF;*.JPX;*.JP2;*.J2C;*.J2K;*.JPC)
JPEG Stereo (*.JPS)
Multi-Picture Format (*.MPO)
PCX (*.PCX)
Photoshop PDF (*.PDF;*.PDP)
Photoshop Raw (*.RAW)
Pixar (*.PXR)
PNG (*.PNG;*.PNS)
Portable Bit Map (*.PBM;*.PGM;*.PPM;*.PNM;*.PFM;*.PAM)
Scitex CT (*.SCT)
Targa (*.TGA;*.VDA;*.ICB;*.VST)
TIFF (*.TIF;*.TIFF)

3

4

Coloring and formatting images

PHOTOSHOP ALLOWS YOU TO UPLOAD different formats of graphic files, from traditional jpeg, bmp, or gif files, to those belonging to other programs such as png, typical of images created with Fireworks, or pdf from Adobe Acrobat. The psd format is the standard for images created or manipulated with Photoshop, and even if the size of the file increses, it retains all the stages of image manipulation.

1. Begin the exercise with one of the sample images from Windows, which you will open in Photoshop. Since you will make several changes to the color, it is important to create a copy of this file. Open the **File** menu and choose **Save As**.

2. In the **Save As** box, select the **Photoshop PSD** format in the **Format** field.

3. Navigate to the images or pictures folder on your computer and press the **Save** button.

4. You will make some modifications to the base color of the image. Click on the **Image** menu and click on the **Mode** option.

The **Save As** command from the **File** menu opens the dialog box of the same name, where you must establish a name for the new document and indicate the format in which to store the image.

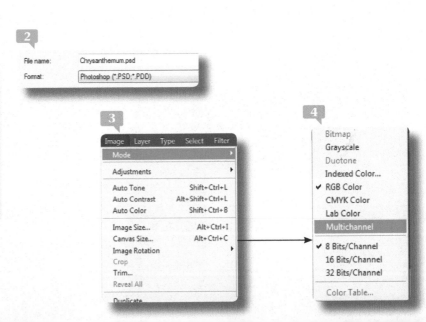

5. So that all the color options are active, it is desirable to have RGB images and 8 Bits/Channel. Generally, the program will open all files with this setup, but if you wish, you may modify these options. Choose the **Multichannel** color mode.

6. Note that in the Multichannel mode, image enhances the warm channels. Pull back the **Image** menu, click on the **Mode** option and select **Lab Color.**

7. The selected mode adds extra image brightness, as is used for working with Photo CD images, as well as to edit the luminance and color values of an image separately. To return the image to its previous state, press the key combination **Ctrl + Z.**

8. Finally, change the image to grayscale. Before you open the **Image** menu, click on the **Mode** option and select **RGB Color** option to return to the original image.

9. Re-open the **Image** menu, click the **Mode** option and select the **Grayscale** option.

10. Since the selected option will remove the colors of the image, the program asks for confirmation to continue with the process. Press the **Discard** button.

11. Check that the image now shows the new color state. To return to the original colors, close the image without saving the changes. Press the small x of the tab image and in the dialog box that appears, click **No.**

Message

Discard color information?

To control the conversion, use Image > Adjustments > Black & White.

[Discard]   [Cancel]

☐ Don't show again

When converting a color image to **grayscale**, the program will be prompted to discard the color information.

Creating images

IN ADDITION TO WORKING ON IMAGE FILES, in order to modify and make appropriate adjustments, you can also choose to create new images from scratch and work on them using the various drawing tools and tweaks that Photoshop offers. All parameters that were assigned when creating a new file can be modified later. The creation of new images is carried out from the file menu or through a combination of relevant keystrokes. The assignment of parameters is done in the new dialog box.

1. To begin, pull down the **File** menu and click **New**.

2. The display now shows the **New** dialog box. First, assign a name to the new image. In the **Name** field, type the term you want. 🔲

3. In the next field, **Preset**, you can adjust the settings for different aspects of the new image: from the paper size that will be used should you decide to print, to the resolution. You will change the default measurements of the image. Double-click in the **Width** field and type **15**. 🔲

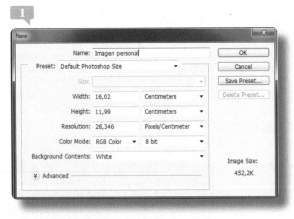

Access the **New** box from the **File** menu or by pressing the Ctrl + N and choose a name for your new document.

4. Then click the arrow in the field that shows the term **Centi-meters** and, after consulting the measurement units available, make sure that centimeters are selected by default.

5. Notice that the **Preset** field now shows **Custom** as the term because of the changed entry. Now double-click in the **Height** field and enter the value **10**.

6. In this exercise, you won't modify the resolution or the color mode. Because of its complexity, these will be discussed later. However, you will assign a transparent background color for the canvas. Choose the **Transparent** option in the **Background contents** field.

7. Before finishing, click the button in the **Advanced** section to verify that the color profile of the image and pixel aspect ratio can be changed.

8. You can confirm that the image has been created. It is very important to note this process does not involve storing the image in the system, so that when the program is closed at this point the document disappears. Click the **OK** button and watch what happens on the screen.

IMPORTANT

If you want all your new documents to have the same properties, you can save the values you set in the New box using the **Save Preset** button. After saving the setting it will appear with the name you gave it in the Preset field.

You can choose among a white background color, selected by default, transparent, or you can select a color from the palette.

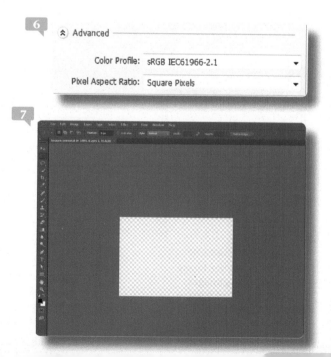

Modifying the size of the image

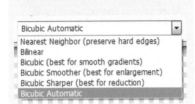
ANY PARAMETER ASSIGNED DURING THE CREATION of a new image can subsequently be changed, once the image is in the work area. To change its size, the program offers a unique dialog box, called Image size, where it is possible to change both the values and the units of measure.

1. The objective of this lesson is to change the size of the file created in the previous exercise. To begin, open the **Image** menu and choose **Image Size.**

2. This feature can be modified according to two conditions: the pixel dimensions of the image or the percentage relative to the current size. Let's do a test. Click the arrow button in the list box with the word **Pixel** corresponding to the field **Width** in pixels in the **Dimensions** section and choose **Percent.**

3. The image is fixed in a proportion of 100%. In the **Width** field enter the value **200.**

4. The **Height** field has changed at the same time as the **Width** field due to the link between them. In the next section

Open the dialog box **Image Size** by using the **Image** menu option. Then select Percent in the section Dimensions in pixels.

010

Document size, you can directly modify the physical dimensions of the image: the width and the height. These two fields are also linked. Click the check box **Constrain Proportions** to disable it.

5. Notice that the two symbols of connection, both the **Pixel Dimensions** section and the **Document size** section, have disappeared. Next, you will modify only the width of the image, without affecting the height. In the **Width** field of the **Document Size** section enter the value 20.

6. The field containing the measurement unit, which by default is set to inches, contains other units (picas, inches, points, millimeters...). The **Resolution** field contains the screen resolution that is best suited to the size of the image to provide the best quality at all times. Press the **Auto...** button.

7. The **Auto Resolution** box opens, where the resolution is shown proportional to the pixel dimensions. In the **Quality** section you can assign the level of image quality, as applicable. This quality is by default **Good**, although you can choose the options **Best** or **Draft**, whwen thinking about printing the image. Click **Cancel** to close this box and click **OK** to accept changes and terminate the exercise.

6

OK
Cancel
Auto...

Pressing the **Auto** button opens the Auto Resolution box, where you can change the resolution of the image and choose from three levels of quality.

4

☑ Scale Styles
☐ Constrain Proportions
☑ Resample Image:
    Bicubic Automatic

When you turn off the **Constrain Proportions** option, you can manually and independently change the width and height of the image.

7

Auto Resolution   ✕

Screen: 52,362   Lines/Centimeter ▼   OK
                                  Cancel
┌ Quality ───────────
│ ○ Draft   ◉ Good   ○ Best

8

5

┌ Document Size: ─────────────
Width: 20| Centimeters ▼
Height: 19,97   Centimeters ▼
Resolution: 28,346   Pixels/Centimeter ▼

Modifying the dimensions of the canvas

THE CANVAS IS THE WORKSPACE where an image is located and can be subsequently retouched and manipulated. Altering the size of the canvas does not in any way change the image size. Photoshop offers the user the canvas size command, which lets you change the dimensions of the working space around the image. Should the canvas size be increased, it will appear as the same color as the background image assigned at the time of its creation.

1. In this exercise, you are going to change the size of the canvas of a file. To start, open the simple image **011.jpg** in Photoshop. It can be downloaded from our website, and a copy stored in your pictures folder. Once opened, pull down the menu **Image** and select the **Canvas Size** option. 🔲

2. The display shows the dialog box **Canvas size**. On top of that dialog box, you can see the current size of the canvas: the width and the height. In the **New Size** section, you introduce the new values. Double-click in the **Width** field and type the value 10. 🔲

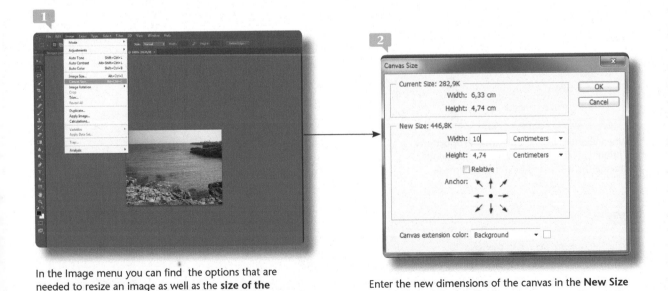

In the Image menu you can find the options that are needed to resize an image as well as the **size of the canvas** where it is located.

Enter the new dimensions of the canvas in the **New Size** box section of Canvas Size.

3. In this case, to adjust the characteristics of our sample image, assign a lower value for the height. Double-click in the **Height** field and enter the value **8**.

4. The **Anchor** scheme, which is located at the bottom of the dimensions fields, determines where in the resized canvas you can find the existing image. By default, according to the visual pattern, the image would be at the center of the canvas. To change this position, simply click on the appropriate arrow in the invisible grid. Let's test it. Click the center arrow to the right of this scheme.

5. The image would be located, in this case, on the right-hand side of the canvas, leaving the left blank. Indicate that you want the image positioned on the top left. Click the top left of the diagram.

6. Let's accept the new canvas size. Click the **OK** button and verify that the image has been placed in the upper left corner of the canvas and the piece of canvas that was added is white, the default color for the background when creating new documents.

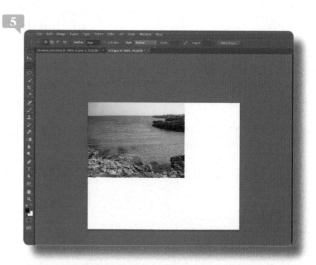

You can see better how the changes in canvas size affects your document if you have an image open in Photoshop. Note that if the dimensions of the canvas are smaller than the image, the program displays a warning message informing you that the image has been cropped.

Cropping images

CROPPING IS THE PROCESS OF REMOVING parts of an image to create focus or to strengthen the composition. Photoshop has several methods for cropping images. One of them, which is described in this exercise, is to use the tool and the command Crop, the first of which is found in the tool palette and the second in the Image menu. Another way is to separate crop images surrounding transparent pixels or background color pixels which is specified by using the Trim command.

1. In this exercise you will be shown how to crop an image to discard those parts or areas of it that aren't wanted. You will carry out this exercise with a new sample file, **012.jpeg**. It can be downloaded from our website and saved to your Pictures folder. Once you have it, open it in the Photoshop workspace.

2. The **Crop Tool** is in fifth place in the Tools palette. Click on it to activate it.

3. A new addition to this version of the program is when activating the **Crop Tool** a dashed frame appears around the entire image. Previously, the user had to trace the framework by using the drag technique. The **Crop Tool** has been improved in general: new commands and functions have been added.

012

Another innovation is the possibility of changing the orientation of the trimming frame. Simply click on the icon that shows a curved arrow to the left of the command **Straighten**. 2

4. Now you will attemp to resize the crop frame or place the image you want to keep inside it. In this case, click on the image, hold the mouse button, drag it to the boat in the photo that lies more or less on the center of the trimming frame. 3

5. The two empty fields located in the Options Bar **Crop Tool** let you specify the exact dimensions of the trimming frame, while the field to the left of them that contains the term **Unconstrained**, offers a choice of different percentages of appearance which have been predefined for the frame. 4 The **Straighten** command allows you to straighten a crooked image by drawing a straight line as a guide. The **View** field allows to you to change the type where the guidelines are displayed over the image clip. In this version of the program, many new options have been added (previously there was only a **Rule of Thirds** and a **Grid**). Display this field and, after checking all the options available, choose for example the so-called **Triangle**. 5

6. Complete this exercise by clicking on the **Commit current crop operation**, which displays a check mark in the right area to confirm the trimming options. 6

Cropping in perspective

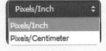
SOMETIMES, WHEN TAKING PHOTOGRAPHS of buildings or tall landmarks, the perspective can give poor, unwanted and unsatisfactory results. It is for such cases that Adobe has added a new trimming function, called Perspective Crop, whereby, after the relevant manual settings, the program deals with correcting the problems of perspective, making the appropriate calculations to obtain a better picture.

1. To carry out this exercise we recommend that you download sample file **013.jpg** from our website, although you can use your own image in the same style. When you have the photograph you want to use, open it in the Photoshop workspace. 〔1〕

2. Rather than correct the image, you will show what effects may be applied with the new **Perspective Crop Tool** in Photoshop CS6. In the Tools panel, click on the arrowhead of the **Crop Tool** and click on **Perspective Crop Tool.** 〔2〕

3. Once the tool has been activated, you should proceed by inserting the necessary points to manually create a grid on which

013

to base the cuts in perspective. This time, you will try to crop the image so as to display the top half of the tower without perspective. Start by clicking the first desired point: the upper left corner of the building, then do the same in the top right corner.

4. The width exceeding the trimming frame should be approximately the same as the width exceeding the building. Now click approximately half way down the right wall of the building to insert a new point for cropping, then insert a new point at the opposite end.

5. When inserting the fourth point, the grid appears clearly, while the rest of the image, the part that will be discarded after the cut, is shown as pale in color. Before the cut, indicate that the options in the Options Bar **Perspective Crop Tool** are the same as the settings for the **Crop Tool** in earlier versions of the application. Thus, you can indicate some exact measurements for the crop area and the resolution of the resulting image. Click the button **Front Image**.

6. The resulting image will have the same characteristics in terms of size and resolution as the original. To check the result of cropping in perspective, press the confirmation button bar options.

IMPORTANT

The Clear command in the Options Bar of the Perspective Crop Tool lets you remove the parameters you added by using the **Front Image** command. In turn the Show Grid Overlay option allows you to hide the divisions of the grid cut, leaving only the frame.

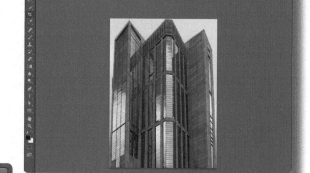

Front Image

By pressing the **Front Image** button, the width, height, and resolution fields in the Options Bar are automatically filled.

Applying content-based scaling

IMPORTANT

Keep in mind that the **Content-Aware Scale** command can't be applied to adjustment, mask, 3D or video layers, several layers simultaneously, or groups of layers.

PHOTOSHOP OFFERS AN INTERESTING FEATURE that allows you to establish a scale based on the content of the image, which will automatically recompose an image when resized. With this function, the most important areas are retained as the image adapts to its new dimensions, so you will not have to waste time on cropping or retouching.

1. This exercise will show the difference between scaling an image based on the content and scaling it normally. To do this, use image **014.jpg**, which can be downloaded from our website and stored in the picture folder. Once you have it stored, open it in Photoshop.

2. In order to transform an image composed of a single background layer,  you have to convert it to a normal layer to be able to unlock it. We will discuss layers in more detail later in this book, but for now, just convert this to a normal layer.

3. In the **Layers** panel, drag the current layer **Background** to the second icon on the right located at the bottom of the panel, 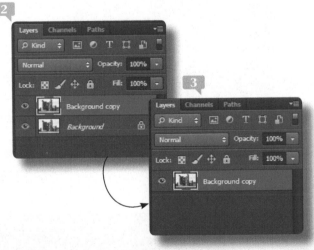 then delete the **Background** layer by selecting it and pressing the **Delete** key.

If the image you are going to scale has only one layer and this is the background, you must first convert it to a regular layer, for which you can use the **Background from layer** from the context menu.

4. To continue, open the **Edit** menu, and click the option **Content-Aware Scale.**

5. In the margins of the image, there will be some handles that allow you to modify the horizontal and vertical scales. Click on the central handle on the right, and pull it toward the left until the width of the image is established at 80% (you can see this value in the **Options Bar**).

6. As you see, the image will automatically recompose as you change its width, keeping it in perfect condition and maintaining the proportion of the major areas. As always when working with transformation tools, it is possible to change the scale by applying new values in the **Options Bar.** In this case, besides the values for height, width, and position of the image, you can define the threshold for the scale based on the content in order to minimize distortion, select a channel to specify what areas to protect, and enable protection for skin tones. Apply the transformation by clicking the icon showing a check mark in the **Options Bar.**

7. To finish this simple exercise, pull down the **File** menu and select **Save.**

014

IMPORTANT

By default, the function **Content-Aware Scale** applies a threshold value to prevent 100% distortion, select a channel to specify which areas should be protected and that you have disabled the protection of skin tones.

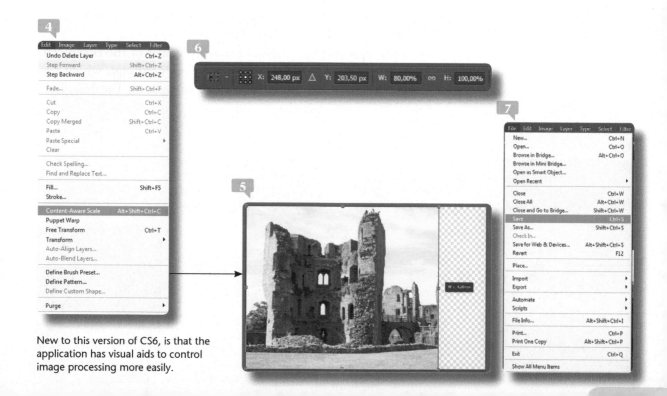

New to this version of CS6, is that the application has visual aids to control image processing more easily.

Adjusting the colors of an image

THE CURVE ADJUSTMENT OPTIONS are necessary for adjusting lighting, shadows, and midtones of an image. The graph shows this adjustment as a diagonal line: at the top shows the degree of illumination, in the central part, halftones, and at the bottom, the amount of shadows. On the other side, the color balance adjustment lets you adjust and correct the colors of an image, enhancing the colors red, blue, or green or adding cyan, magenta, or yellow.

1. To start, you will modify the levels of shadows and lighting of image **015.jpg** with the **Curves** adjustment tool. In the **Adjustments** pane, click on the third setting available.

2. If you make adjustments to your images from the **Adjustments** panel instead of from the menu **Image/Adjustments**, you will create new adjustment layers that are added to the background layer. In the **Properties** panel load properties and applied settings. The upper graph shows the degree of lighting, central, and midtones, while the lower shows the amount of shade in the image. The horizontal and vertical axes represent the original intensity values of the pixels. The diagonal line represents the central axis through which you can visually modify the quantity of light in the image.

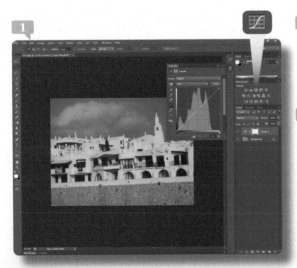

015

Click the bottom right of the third box from the top of the first column. 🔲

3. The line makes a curve from the point previously marked, while the image has been lightened. To lighten it a bit more, click the top left of the first box from the top of the last column. 🔲

4. Next, you will modify the color of the image by using the **Color Balance**. In the **Adjustments** pane, click on the icon showing a set of scales. 🔲

5. Now the **Properties** panel shows the values of the channels cyan, magenta, and yellow on one side, and red, green, and blue on the other. As an example, drag the first slider toward the red channel. 🔲

6. To decrease the blue tones, drag the **Yellow-Blue** slider toward the yellow side.

7. You can perform the same operation so that it only affects the part of the object that is illuminated by activating the **Highlights** option. The biggest advantage of working from the settings panel is that the editing of the images is not destructive, since it takes place, as we said, in layers. To end the exercise we will show you how to override any of these applied settings, for example, relating to the color balance. To do this, simply drag the relevant adjustment layer, which displays the text **Color Balance 1**, until the icon at the bottom of the layers panel that shows a trash can.

IMPORTANT

Photoshop offers a number of predetermined curves that can be applied to achieve different effects on an image. As an example, the adjustment **Invert** creates a reverse negative effect on the photograph.

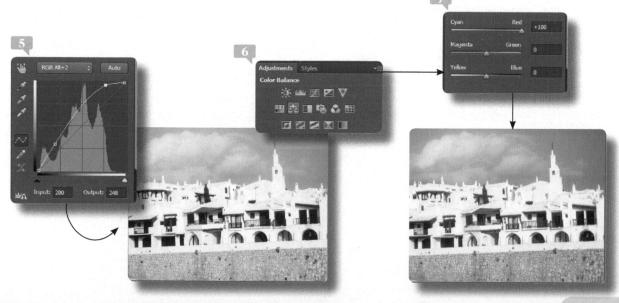

Equalizing, mixing colors and gradients

EQUALIZATION REORGANIZES THE BRIGHTNESS values of images automatically. By performing this action, the program regulates the brightness of the image based on the existing colors, redistributing uniformly intermediate pixel values from gray scale meanwhile, the channel mixer allows the colors of an image to be adjusted from the existing primary colors. With respect to the gradient, Photoshop has sixteen different types of compound gradients with different colors that can be reversed.

1. To perform this exercise, use an image showing a variety of colors (you may use image **016.jpg** that can be found in the download area of our website). First, we will show you how to equalize the colors. Open the **Image** menu, click the **Adjustments** command and select **Equalize**.

2. This command automatically rearranges the brightness values of the current image. Pull down the **Edit** menu and click the option **Undo Equalize**

3. Next, we'll show you how to manipulate the colors of an image channel. In the **Adjustments** pane, click on the next to last icon in the second row.

Remember that you can easily make any adjustments from the **Adjustments** panel, given that the program will add the layers of the selected settings to the Background layer.

4. The channel mixer adjusts the colors using different color channels of the available colors to create high quality images in grayscale, sepia tone, or other tints, and creative color adjustments. Double-click the **Green** field and type, for example, the value **146.**

5. Positive values decrease the channel, while negative values increase it. To increase the color blue, double-click its field and type, for example, the value **-150.**

6. To restore the original appearance of the image, delete the adjustment layer channel mixer by clicking the trash can icon that appears in the **Layers** panel and click the **Delete** button in the confirmation box that appears.

7. The last thing we will do is adjust the color gradient. Click the last icon in the **Settings** pane, the **Gradient Map** adjustment.

8. This setting has the necessary options to manipulate the degree of gradient of certain default colors for Photoshop. The gradient that appears by default is the combination of colors that are currently selected as the foreground color and background color. Click on the **Invert** option in the **Properties** panel.

9. Click the arrow button, which shows the current gradient and choose one by clicking any of the available samples.

10. Finish the exercise by eliminating the adjustment layer to restore the original appearance of the image.

Converting color images to black and white

PHOTOSHOP PROVIDES A TOOL THAT EASILY converts color images to sophisticated black and white images. With the black and white tool you can create monochrome images and adjust tonal values and tints quickly and easily. It also offers a gallery of presets that simulate colored filters —high-contrast, neutral density, and infrared— as well as let you create and save custom settings.

1. By modifying the color sliders featuring black and white settings, you will apply a sepia tone to image **016.jpg**, which you amended in the previous exercise. To begin, click the third icon on the second row of the **Adjustments** panel, which corresponds to the previously mentioned task.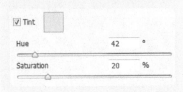

2. The program applies default values to convert the image to black and white. Let's look at some of the presets. Click the arrow button for the **Black & White** field, then select, for example, the yellow filter.

3. Notice how the appearance of the image and color values change. Press **Auto** to return to the default monochrome setting.

IMPORTANT

Keep in mind that if you convert an image to black and white using the **Black and white** dialog box, instead of the Adjustments panel, you can also directly modify the tone and hue saturation applied to the effect.

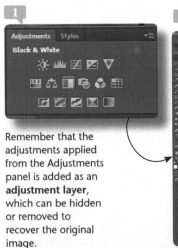

Remember that the adjustments applied from the Adjustments panel is added as an **adjustment layer**, which can be hidden or removed to recover the original image.

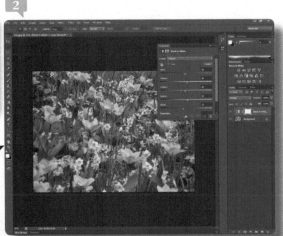

4. Then, as we said, you will change the color sliders and apply a touch of color to add a sepia effect to the image. Write the value **50** in the red regulator percentage field and **120** in the yellow one.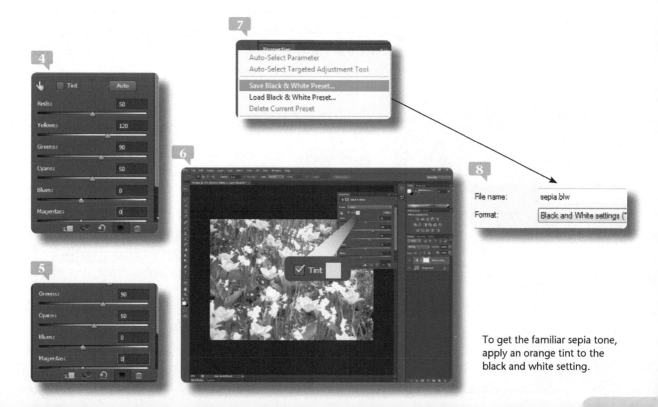

5. In the **Greens** field enter **90**, and in cyan **50**.

6. Double-click in the blue percentage regulator field and insert the value **0**, and in magenta enter the value **0**.

7. Once you have changed the colors, apply a tint to get a sepia tone. Click the check box to activate the **Tint** option.

8. The image now shows a sepia tone as well. Once the desired result is achieved, save the configuration to use it whenever you need to. Click the Options button in the Properties panel and then click the **Save Black & White Preset**.

9. As you see, the custom settings of black and white by default are saved in the folder **Black and White** in Photoshop with the .BLW extension. In the **Save** box **Name** field enter the term you want and press the **Save** button.

10. To finish this exercise, save a copy of the image with the name **Sepia**.

017

IMPORTANT

The Black & White feature, included in the Image menu command Adjustments and in the Adjustments panel, features six color sliders, RGB and CMY can be graduated from –200 to 300%. These regulators are adjustable between –200% and 300%, a total of 300 gives a result just as bright as the original.

To get the familiar sepia tone, apply an orange tint to the black and white setting.

Creating basic selections

IMPORTANT

The edges of a selection can be smoothed or rounded. To do this, you must modify the settings of **fading** and **smoothing**. Fading can blur the edges, reducing the transition boundary between image and the frame selection. This is an effect that creates gradual color differences without being too noticeable.

PHOTOSHOP LETS YOU SELECT any part of the image using numerous selection tools. To select specific parts, rectangular or circular tracing tools are used: the Rectangular Marquee and the Elliptical Marquee. These tools allow you to draw a rectangle, ellipse, rounded rectangle, row, column, and column of single pixels.

1. First, select an image area to change, such as its colors. Image **018.jpg** can be used, and can be found in the download area of our website. You can store it in your images folder. Select the **Rectangular Marquee Tool**, which is the second in the **Tools** panel.

2. The **Options Bar**, located under the **Menu Bar** shows the characteristics of the active tool. Keep them as they appear and, by dragging, select a rectangular area in the image.

3. The selected part, which is at present outlined by a dashed line, can be treated independently. Click the arrow that appears at the corner of the twelfth tool in the **Tools** panel, and choose the **Paint Bucket**. To paint the selection with the foreground color, click inside it.

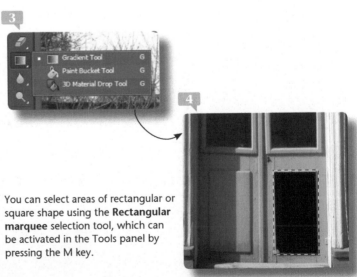

You can select areas of rectangular or square shape using the **Rectangular marquee** selection tool, which can be activated in the Tools panel by pressing the M key.

4. To deselect the selected image, click the **Select** menu and click the **Deselect** option.

5. You can also perform this action by pressing **Ctrl + d**. The selection tool can also remove part of an image. Enable the rectangular selection tool again, draw another area by dragging a rectangular selection, and press the **Delete** key.

6. When you delete a selection, the **Fill** box opens. Here you can choose how you want to fill the selection you are going to delete. You will get to know this fill content utility in greater detail later. In this case, press the arrow button on the **Use** field, select the **Foreground Color** 5 then press the **OK** button.

7. In the **Tools** panel, click the arrow that appears at the bottom right corner of the **Rectangular Marquee Tool** and select the **Elliptical Marquee Tool**. 6

8. Trace, by dragging an elliptical selection area at any point in the image. 7

9. Now you will modify some aspect of color selection, which by default is transparent. In the Adjustments pane, click the first setting **Brightness/Contrast**.

10. In the **Properties** pane, click the right-hand side of the slider bar for the brightness and press **OK**. 8

018

IMPORTANT

Holding down the **Shift** key while creating the framework for selection creates regular forms, ie, squares or circles, depending on the tool you are using.

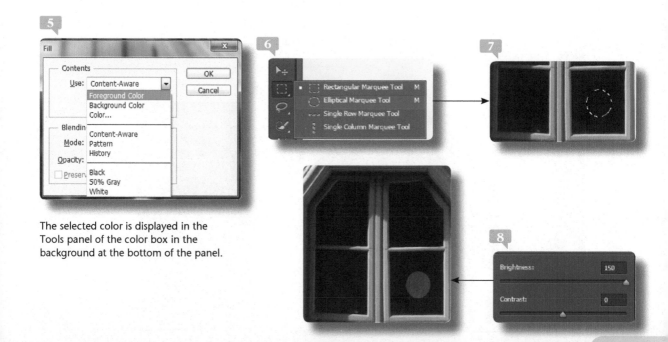

The selected color is displayed in the Tools panel of the color box in the background at the bottom of the panel.

Freehand selection

1. THE LASSO TOOL ALLOWS YOU TO DRAW A FREEHAND selection area by marking an initial anchor point, drawing the area you want to select by dragging back to the starting point. The **Polygonal Lasso Tool** is used to draw a selection area by inserting as many anchor points as necessary. In this case, to close the selection, you must put the last anchor point on top of the first. The **Magnetic Lasso Tool** allows you to draw a selection area by bordering the item you want to select. Photoshop inserts the appropriate anchoring points depending on the color change of the element.

2. To begin, click the **Lasso Tool**, 🔲 the third in the **Tools** panel, and by dragging, draw a selection area on your image, which is closed by clicking on the first anchor point again.

3. The selected element is outlined by a dashed line. 🔲 At this point you can make any change that affects only this part of the image. To deselect, press the key combination **Ctrl + D**.

4. The application of the **Lasso** selection tool is fairly complicated due to the precision with which the outline must be carried out. The **Polygonal Lasso Tool** can solve this problem. Click the arrow that appears on the **Lasso Tool** and select the previously mentioned tool. 🔲

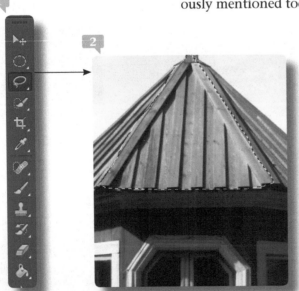

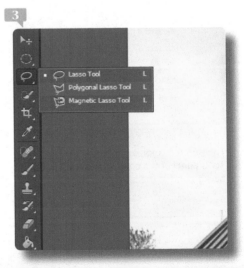

019

5. Start by applying the first anchor point. Click anywhere on your image.

6. This tool lets you apply different anchor points so that it is not necessary to perform the selection drawing freehand. You can insert as many anchor points as you want. Do this to create your selection area, close it by cicking once on the initial anchor point.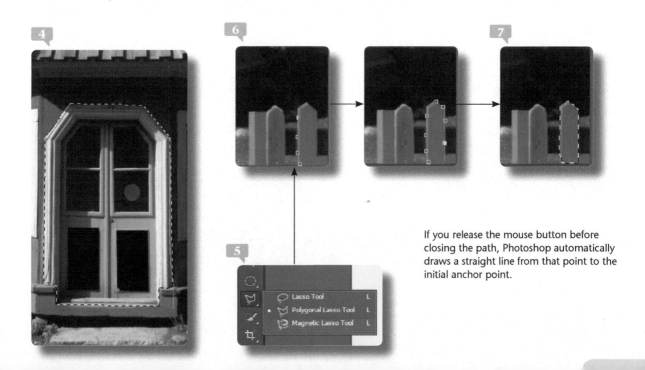

7. Once the selection area is defined, it can be modified in many ways. To unselect press the **Ctrl + D**.

8. Finally, you will learn to use the **Magnetic Lasso**, which draws a selection area without inserting anchor points since the program itself selects its own anchor points based on the color of the enclosed area. Press the arrow of the **Polygonal Lasso** tool and select the **Magnetic Lasso Tool**.

9. This tool is very useful for selecting objects with complex edges in high-contrast backgrounds. So that Photoshop alone traces the selection area that interests you, first create an anchor point and slowly pass the mouse pointer around the edges, without pressing the mouse button.

10. To close the selection, you must insert a last anchor point, which coincides with the first.

If you release the mouse button before closing the path, Photoshop automatically draws a straight line from that point to the initial anchor point.

Selecting with the Magic Wand

1. USE THE MAGIC WAND TOOL to select an area of an image with a range of similar colors based on the stated level. This tool, like any other selection tool, allows you to combine different selections by activating the Add to selection of the Options Bar. To deselect one of the additions, you can activate the **Subtract from selection** command. There is also the **Intersect with selection** command, which selects only the common part of two delineated areas.

2. To perform this exercise you can use the example image **020.jpg** which is found in the download area of our website. Click the arrowhead of the fourth tool in the **Tools** panel and select the **Magic Wand Tool.**

3. The cursor now becomes a magic wand. The higher the level of tolerance, the more flexible Photoshop will be when selecting areas for tones and colors. Double-click the field **Tolerance** in the **Options Bar**, enter the value **80** and press **Return.**

4. Uncheck **contiguous** to select non-continous areas and, if using **020.jpg**, click on one of the petals and see what happens.

Select the **Magic Wand Tool**, set its properties (tolerance, smoothing, etc.). In the Options Bar take into account the characteristics of the image you are practicing on and see how it responds by clicking anywhere on it.

5. Photoshop has automatically identified a selection area with similar colors to the point where you clicked. To reduce the area of selection you can perform two actions: decrease the tolerance or subtract the portion of the selection. However, this does not always give the expected result if the tolerance is still too high. In this case, press **Ctrl + D** to delete the current selection.

6. Then double-click the **Tolerance** field in the **Options Bar**, enter the value **20** and press **Return**.

7. See how the tool now works by clicking on any orange petal: only a part of the petals are selected.

8. Reassign a higher tolerance to reselect all the petals.

9. Now you will obscure the selection. In the **Adjustments** pane, click the second icon, which is the **Levels** adjustment.

10. You can see in the **Layers** panel that an adjustment layer that affects only the selection has been created. Double-click on the central field of the input levels, corresponding to the midtones, and enter the value **0,4**.

11. Imagine the possibilities of this tool in terms of photo retouching. You will end this exercise by removing the adjustment layer you just added. Double-click on the Trash icon in the **Layers** panel, confirming the action in the two boxes.

Tolerance: 20

Adding and subtracting selections

IMPORTANT

To reselect the last selection made, use the **Reselect** option from the **Select** menu.

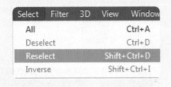

THE OPTIONS BAR FOR THE MAGIC WAND TOOL provides three commands to manage the selections made with this tool: Add to Selection, Subtract from Selection, and Intersect with Selection. Even when the tolerance level is set to very high, it may be that the program includes parts of the image that we want to select or, conversely, leaves out of the selection a fragment that should be included. In such cases, the commands mentioned previously allow manipulation of the selection by adding or removing items.

1. To perform this exercise, **021.jpg** can be used if desired. It can be found on the download area of our website. With the **Magic Wand Tool** selected and a tolerance value of **50**, [1] click one of the panels of the balloon. [2]

2. Imagine you want to select all the stripes of that color. In the Options Bar, click the third icon, which is the **Add to Selection** command. [3]

3. From now on, any part of the image on which you click will be added to the current selection. Try it. [4]

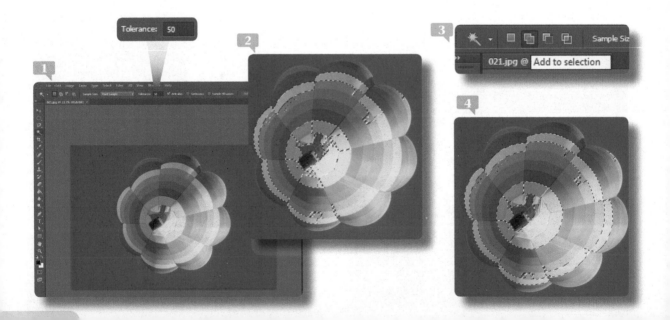

4. When you need to make changes in choices, we recommend that you use the **Zoom Tool** to increase the visibility of the affected area and thus work more accurately. Now activate the **Brightness/Contrast** adjustment in the **Adjustments** panel and move the Brightness control slider to the right to increase this value. 5

5. Note that the Layers panel, which corresponds to the adjustment layer, displays only the selected image fragment. 6 The action contrary to adding selections is, obviously, subtracting selections. To show the application of the Subtract from Selection command, you will, in the first place, make a new selection on the image. Move to the **Background** layer and with the **Magic Wand Tool**, click on any bar of the balloon. 7

6. Verify that the **Add to Selection** is enabled in the Options Bar and click on another strip of the same color. 8

7. What you want to do now is to remove part of the selection. Click the **Subtract from Selection** command in the Options Bar, which is located below the one that you have just used. 9 Now click on one of the selections. 10

8. As always, you could apply color, soften, or take any other action on the selected area. Press the key combination **Ctrl.+ D** to delete the settings, and the key combination **Ctrl + S** to save the image as .psd.

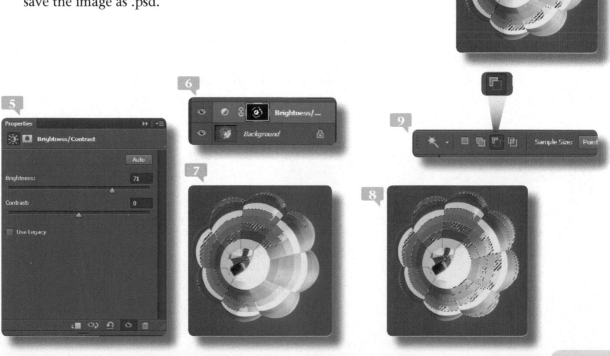

Selecting and painting at the same time

THE QUICK SELECTION TOOL LETS YOU QUICKLY MAKE selections. It's used for painting a selection with a configurable round brush tip and to loosely draw the image area by dragging while the quick selection tool automatically completes the selection, expanding outward and following the defined edges of the image. This tool complements the function Refine Edge, which allows further adjustment of the selection boundary to improve the quality or view the selection against different backgrounds or skin mode for easy editing.

1. To perform this exercise you can use the image **022.jpg** which is found in the download area of our website. To begin, click the arrowhead of the **Magic Wand Tool** and select the **Quick Selection Tool.**

2. This tool also offers a **New selection** function (enabled by default), **Add to selection,** and **Subtract from selection.** Before using it, reduce the brush size. You can do this by pressing the left square bracket on your keyboard or by changing the value of the brush size. Click the arrow for brush selector in the Options Bar.

3. From here you can modify the main features of the brush, such as the diameter and hardness. Double-click the **Size** field, enter the value **15** then press **Return.**

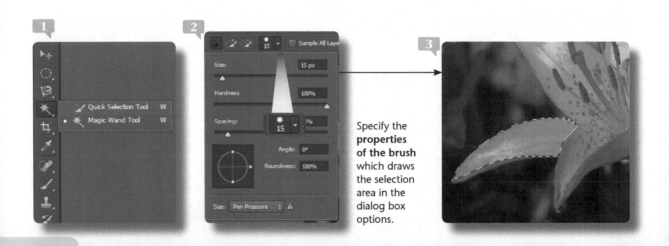

Specify the **properties of the brush** which draws the selection area in the dialog box options.

4. To create the quick pick, click a flower petal and drag gently until it is completely selected.

5. Verify that the paint around the edges of a shape, the selection area, extends to follow its contours. You can also create the selection area by clicking on several points close to those that were added in the initial selection. Now click on **Refine Edge** in the **Options Bar.**

6. You can also access this box from the **Select** menu. To create a more accurate selection boundary zone with smooth transitions or fine detail, the radius should be increased. This in turn, focuses the edge contrast of the selection eliminating fuzzy defects and providing sharpness. Double-click the **Contrast** field and enter the value **80.**

7. The **Smooth** control is used to reduce irregular border areas of the selection and softens contours while the **Feather** control creates soft-edged transitions between the selection and surrounding pixels. Finally, the **Shift Edge** option will reduce or increase the edge limit of the selection. To expand the selection, enter the value **50** in this field.

8. You can preview the effect of the changes before applying them permanently. In the **View Mode** section, there are different options for changing the selection display mode. Press the arrow button and select the **View** field, for example, the **On Black** option.

9. Remember that you can restore the original appearance of the selection edges by checking the **Show Original** box. Click the **OK** button to save the settings for the selection and delete the current selection by pressing the key combination **Ctrl + D.**

IMPORTANT

The **Sample All Layers** option from the Options Bar of the Quick Selection Tool must be activated when the image consists of several layers and you want to get a selection of all of them, and not just the currently selected one. For its part, the **Auto-Enhance** option reduces the roughness and solidness of the selection boundary.

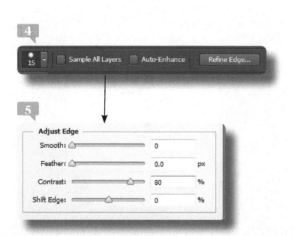

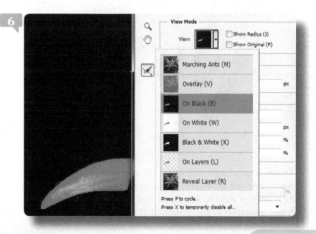

Selecting edges more precisely

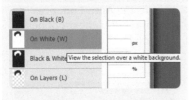
AS SEEN IN THE PREVIOUS EXERCISE, the Refine Edge Tool, which is complementary to the Quick Selection Tool, improves the quality of the edges of a selection and allows you to see that selection on different edges for more simple editing. The Refine Edge box has Refine Radius and Erase Refinements tools that allow you to fine-tune difficult to select edges like hair.

1. In this exercise you will practice the **Refine Edge Tool** to facilitate edge selection. You can use the example image **023. jpg,** which can be found in the download area of our website and which you can store in your images folder. Once you have opened it in Photoshop, follow the previous exercise to select the **Quick Selection Tool** around the boy's hair.

2. Then, access the **Refine Edge** box by pressing the option with the same name in the **Options Bar.**

3. In the **Refine Edge** box, click the arrow button and select **On White** from the **View** field.

To get a good selection you must change the size of the brush and play around with its functions **Add to selection** and **Subtract from selection** in the Options Bar.

4. Zoom on the selection by selecting the **Zoom Tool** and **Refine Edge** box by clicking on the hair (make sure **Zoom in** is enabled for that tool.)

5. Now activate the **Refine Radius** function, whose icon is shown to the left of the **Edge Detection** section, if necessary increase the radius of the brush in the Options Bar and drag around your selection to add precise details of the hair.

6. You can clear the areas that have not been well defined using the new **Erase Refinements Tool**, which can be activated from both the Options Bar as well as in the Refine Edge dialog box. Once activated, drag the brush across the areas that have been improved.

7. Now activate the **Show original** option in the **Refine Edge** box to check the original selection and to compare it to the current image.

8. Finally, press the arrow button in the **Output To** field, select **New Layer** and click **OK**.

9. This has created a new layer containing only the selection you have made. Click on the icon preceding the name of the **Background** layer to show it again here and finish this exercise.

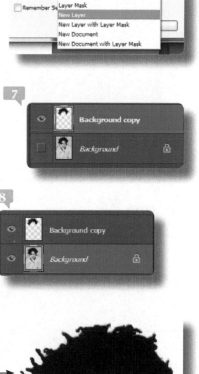

Filling according to content

PHOTOSHOP QUICKLY AND EASILY ALLOWS the removal of elements in an image and to replace them with content that matches the background. To carry out this operation you can use the Delete function when you have made a selection, or the Fill Tool from the Edit menu when a selection has been made. In both cases, the Fill box lets you choose how the selection will be filled.

1. In this exercise you will use the example image **024.jpg** that can be downloaded from our website and stored in your images folder. After opening the image, use one of the selection tools that you have previously learned about, and by adjusting the brush size suitably and playing around with the **Add to selection** and **Subtract from selection** functions, select the man in the picture. ▪ (For best results, choose an area slightly larger than the area you want to replace.)

2. As mentioned in the introduction, after making your selection you can press the **Delete** key or use the **Fill** option in the **Edit** menu to access the **Fill** box. Perform one of these two actions. ▪

You can also access the Fill box by pressing the key combination **Shift + F5**.

3. This opens the **Fill** box, in the **Use** field you must choose what you want to fill the selection with. Click on the arrow in that field and, after checking that, you can also fill the selection with color, a motif, or a defined snapshot —in the **History** panel, select the option **Content-Aware**. ⬛

4. In the section **Blending** you can set the blending mode, which controls the influence of a painting tool or editing of the image pixels and the opacity of the fill. In this case, keep the **Normal** option in the **Mode** field and a percentage of **100%** in the **Opacity** field ⬛ then press the **OK** button to complete the selection at the bottom of the image.

5. Within seconds ⬛ the image is updated: the character disappears and the space is filled uniformly with image content similar to the existing part of the image. Press the key combination **Ctrl + D** to deselect it and see the outcome better. ⬛

6. Although the result is impressive, you could refine it further by removing the traced maroon areas from the child's shirt. To do this, you can use the **Spot Healing Brush Tool**. A later lesson will be devoted to this tool, but for the moment, save these changes.

024

IMPORTANT

It should be noted that the fill depends on the content of a randomly synthesized similar image and, depending on the image used, the results may not be entirely satisfactory. If necessary, follow the menu path **Edit**, **Step Backward**, before removing the selection, to restore the original appearance of the image.

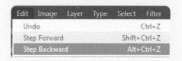

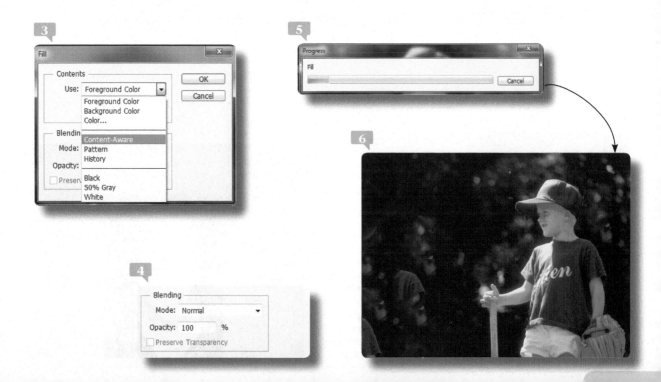

Correcting imperfections

1. TO CORRECT IMPERFECTIONS IN AN IMAGE, Photoshop has the **Healing Brush** Tool, which allows you to copy parts of an image and add them to the image evenly while matching the texture, lighting, and shading of the pixels. To correct bigger imperfections, you should use the **Clone Stamp** Tool, which allows the application of an identical image on a particular area of the canvas.

2. To perform this exercise, you can download sample image **025.jpg** from our website and save it to your images folder. Click the arrow on the **Spot Healing Brush Tool**, the seventh icon in the **Tools** panel, and select the **Healing Brush Tool.**

3. First, you must select the image you want to use, that is, take a sample, and then apply it to the desired area. To take a sample of this image, press to the left of the tonguelip piercing by holding down the **Alt** key. (If you work with the example image, you must set the brush to about 25 pixels or so.)

4. After selecting the image you want to play with, click on the piercing of the tonguelip and see how it disappears.

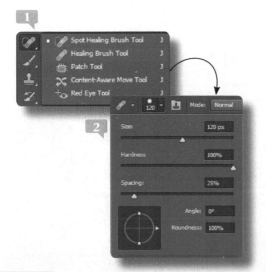

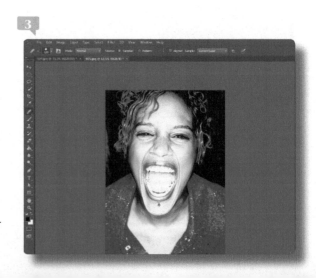

Pressing the **Alt** key when sampling, the pointer becomes a crosshair.

025

5. Then use the clone stamp to remove the fillings. Click on the **Clone Stamp Tool**, the ninth icon in the **Tools** panel.

6. Press the arrow button next to the brush size in the **Options Bar** and set a size of **25** pixels or so.

7. Press **Alt + click** on a tooth without any fillings (the area will be cloned) and then click on the affected teeth to place the copy.

8. From the **Clone Source** palette, you can define up to five different sources of samples for the clone stamp and healing brush. Click the **Window** menu and click the **Clone Source** option.

9. This palette allows us to accurately position the number of samples taken and change the width, height, and angle of rotation of the cloning as well as reverse the direction of a clone source. If you always want to show the layer with the clone source, you must enable the **Show Overlay** option in this palette and set the desired opacity. In this case, hide the palette by pressing the button with a double arrowhead on it's header.

10. The **Clone Stamp Tool** is often used to remove small impurities in images. To finish this exercise, save the retouched image in Photoshop's own **format, .psd**.

IMPORTANT

As we will discuss later, the **Spot Healing Brush Tool** works similarly, with the only difference being that it is not necessary to specify a sample point but that it automatically samples the area around the point to be tweaked.

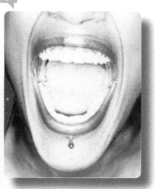

When correcting images is very important to choose the most suitable **diameter** of the brush for each purpose.

Placing patches on an image

THE PATCH TOOL IS USED to correct and repair areas of an image with pixels from another area of the same image. The great virtue of this tool is that by using the area taken as a sample, it retains the texture, lighting, and shading of the original so that, in many cases, the "patch" can be applied subtly. The Smudge Tool is often used in Photoshop for artistic effect: providing a softening or wet effect on the edges.

1. You can use the example image **026.jpg** that can be found in the download area of our website. Click the arrowhead of the **Healing Brush Tool**, the seventh icon in the **Tools** panel and select the **Patch Tool**. 🔲

2. To apply the **Patch Tool**, first you must select the space you want to tweak, that is, where you wish to apply the patch. You should then move the selected area to the part of the image you want to apply the patch to. The selection must be done by hand, using the drag technique. Create a selection area that encompasses the second die next to the letter **Bar** in the image. 🔲

The **Patch Tool** shares space in the Tools panel with the Spot Healing Brush, Healing Brush, and the Red Eye Brush.

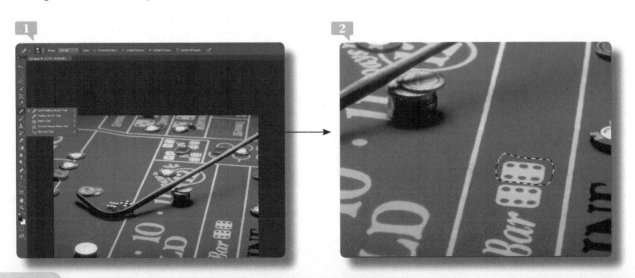

3. To apply the patch you must drag the selection to the area of interest, which is enabled by checking the **Source** option in the Options Bar. You can also select an area to sample and drag it to the repair area with the **Destination** option enabled in the Options Bar. Make sure the **Transparent** option in the Options Bar is disabled.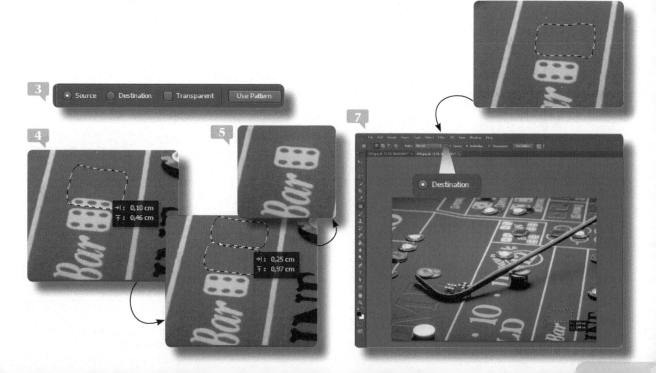

4. Drag the selection until the selected die disappears and then release the mouse button.

5. To check the result, display the **Select** menu and click the **Deselect** option.

6. Then, use the **Patch Tool** to remove the other die.With this tool, draw a selection area, the size of the other die in the area you have just finished retouching.

7. Activate the **Destination** option in the Options Bar of the settings and drag the selection until it is situated on top of the second die, so that it hides it. Release the mouse button and look at the result.

8. Press the key combination **Ctrl + D** to deselect.

9. To finish the exercise, pull down the **File** menu, click on **Save** and keeping the default options selected in the **JPEG Options** box, save the file.

026

IMPORTANT

It is important to know that the **Patch Tool** cannot be used on indexed color images, so if the file you intend to work with is of this type, you must change it using the menu path **Image/Mode/RGB Color**.

✔ 8 Bits/Channel
16 Bits/Channel
32 Bits/Channel

Moving a subject

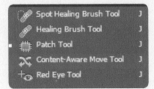

ANOTHER STRIKING ADDITION introduced in this version of Photoshop CS6 is the Content-Aware Move Tool which is included in the correction brushes toolset.With this tool you can relocate objects in an image and duplicate them within the same layer. The Content-Aware Move is used especially for manipulating larger items, regardless of the background they are placed against: the reason is that this very smart tool removes the background against which the object is defined.

1. You will practice with this new motion detection tool on sample file **027.jpeg**. You can download it from our website and save it in your pictures folder. We also suggest that you practice with your own pictures to discover all of the amazing possible results. When the file is available, open it in the work area of the program.

2. The **Content-Aware Move Tool** shares space with the group of editing brushes, so click on the arrow of the **Patch Tool** or **Healing brush Tool** and choose by clicking the appropriate tool. 📝

For best results, it is important to leave a space between the frame selection and the selected item.

027

3. The Options Bar now displays the functions corresponding to the new **Content-Aware Move Tool**. The first group of four are the ones that allow you to manage the selection of items for further manipulation: normal, add, subtract, and intersect. In this case, draw a selection around the athlete, including the oars and the ripple of water. 2

4. The command **Mode** allows you to choose between two options: **Move,** to reposition the selected item in the picture, and **Extend,** to create a duplicate. The special feature of this tool is that it creates a duplicate layer that is placed in the same layer. First you will move the selection slightly. To do this, click on it and drag it to the top of the image. 3

5. When you release the mouse button, the program performs a mixture of the elements contained in the selection and the target area, while eliminating the image from its original position. 4 The result is excellent. Now you will make a couple of copies of the same element. Click the **Mode** menu and click the **Extend** option. 5

6. The **Adaptation** field lets you set the degree of overlap and fidelity at the same time. Display this field and choose **Very Strict.** 6

7. Now click on the selection and drag down to create a first duplicate, repeat the process once more to create three rowers in the same picture. 7

Deleting elements in an image

IMPORTANT

Sometimes, if the element is in contact with another part of the image, it can be difficult to erase. Photoshop has the **Background Eraser Tool**, especially useful when the image is composed of different layers, with which the program automatically deletes the pixels of a layer with transparency by dragging the mouse pointer. This way you can erase the background while keeping the edges of the object in the foreground.

THE PURPOSE OF THE ERASER TOOL, as its name suggests, is to delete any item in the canvas. In the case of existing layers, it will only delete the selected layer, showing the element below, while if it is used with a single image, it will show the bottom of the canvas. The application of the eraser tool is carried out by using the drag technique.

1. Download image **028.jpg** from our website, which you will use for this exercise. Of course, should you wish, you can use your own image. Before using the tool, and since its implementation requires some precision, press Z to activate the **Zoom Tool** and, when satisfied that the **Zoom** function is enabled, double-click on the center of the image.

2. Then, click the **Eraser Tool**, the eleventh icon in the **Tools** panel, which shows a picture of an eraser.

3. With this tool you can change the pixels of an image to the background color or to transparent when the transparency of the layer is not blocked. This tool has three modes: **Brush**, **Pencil**, and **Block**, which can be selected in the **Options Bar**. The properties of the brush can also be modified from the

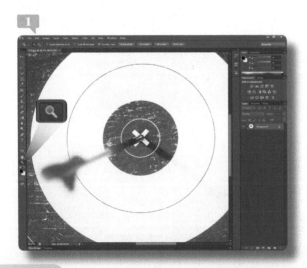

The **Zoom** Tool increases the area of the item you want to delete and therefore allows you to work with more precision.

The Eraser tool shares space in the Tools panel with the tools **Background Eraser** and **Magic Eraser**.

028

options panel. To clear a given area, you must use the drag technique, and remember that you can only retrieve the last fragment deleted. Increase the diameter of the brush to 25 pixels.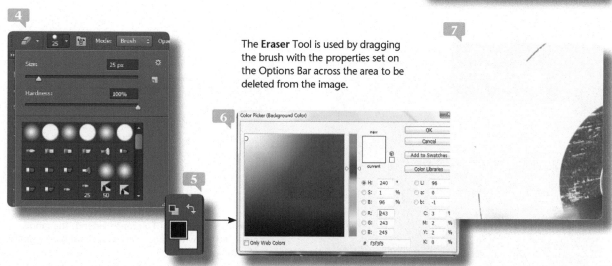

4. Before applying the **Eraser Tool**, change the background color, which by default is white, to the tone of the target. Double-click on white in the **Tools** panel to access the **Color Picker (Background Color)** box.

5. The mouse pointer now takes the form of a dropper and lets you sample a color image. Click the background of the target (see that it is a shade of gray) and press **OK**.

6. Once you have defined the background color to be replaced by the image that you will delete, drag across a portion of the black circle.

7. Effectively, the draft zone changes the background color you have selected. Adjust the properties as necessary and drag across the entire circumference to remove it (use the clone stamp in the red zone that matches the top of the arrow to get a better result).

8. Open the **View** menu and choose **Fit on Screen** to see the final result. Save the image with Photoshop's own format.

The **Eraser** Tool is used by dragging the brush with the properties set on the Options Bar across the area to be deleted from the image.

Removing pixels with the Magic Eraser

SHARING SPACE IN THE TOOLS PANEL with the Eraser Tool and the Background Eraser Tool you will find the Magic Eraser Tool with which you can change all similar pixels to a transparent appearance. Obviously, when working with multiple layers, such transparency will display part of the layer immediately below the selected one.

1. In this exercise, you will get to know the value of the **Magic Eraser Tool**. To do this, you will practice with the sample file **029.psd,** which you can download from our website, and store in the images folder. When you open the file, you can see in the **Layers** panel, layer 0, where the image is located, and another layer, Layer 1, which has created a cloud effect by applying the Clouds filter (you will work with layers and filters later). Click on **Layer 0,** click the arrow on the **Eraser Tool** and then choose the **Magic Eraser Tool.**

2. As with the selection tools, the Options Bar for the **Magic Eraser Tool** lets you specify a tolerance value to define the color range to be deleted. In this case, enter the value 55 in the **Tolerance** field of the **Options Bar.**

Remember that a high **Tolerance** extends the range of colors and a low tolerance erases pixels with very similar color values.

3. If the **Anti-alias** option is enabled, the edges of the area to be deleted will appear smooth. Similarly, in order to erase all similar pixels in the image regardless of whether they are adjacent or not, uncheck **Contiguous**. [3]

029

4. The **Sample All Layers** option, meanwhile, can sample the erased color using combined data from all layers. Keep it unchecked. Finally, it is possible to set the opacity to define the intensity of the eraser. In this case, keep the value as 100% so that all pixels are deleted. Click to the right of the basket in the sky, and see what happens. [4]

5. Note that according to the exact point where you press, the results may be slightly different (you can remove more or less pixels). The pixels removed are now transparent, since under the selected layer there is one with a background of clouds, which you now see. Hide Layer 1 by clicking on the eye that appears on the left in the **Layers** panel and verify that the pixels are erased and that now a transparent background is displayed. [5]

6. To finish this simple exercise in which you have seen the enormous usefulness of the **Magic Eraser Tool** and its ease of use, save the resulting image.

IMPORTANT

You can turn erasing tools on (**Eraser, Background Eraser,** and **Magic Eraser**) by pressing the E on your keyboard.

Measuring images

PHOTOSHOP PROVIDES MANY TOOLS designed to help professionals from various fields, such as panoramic photography, medical photography, astrophotography, etc. The measurement function allows users to measure areas defined with the Ruler Tool, with a selection tool or the Count Tool. Depending on the type of data you want included in the measurements log, choose the appropriate tool to use.

1. To perform this exercise continue to work with the file **029.psd**, although you can use any picture you have stored on your computer. To begin, use the **Magnetic Lasso** selection tool to create a selection area and save your measurements. Select it in the **Tools** panel and draw by dragging a selection area around the pole of the basket.

2. To record the measurements of the selected area, pull down the **Window** menu, click the **Measurement Log** command and then press the **Record Measurements** button on the panel.

3. The panel for the Measurement Log reflects the characteristics of the measurement. Note that you can delete the columns you do not need in this panel and resize it and change the order in which the measurements are shown. The column **Sou-**

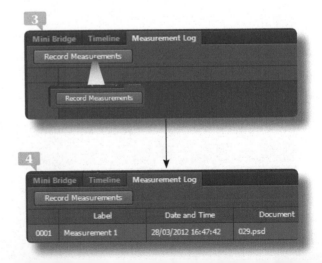

rce shows how measurements have been taken. Let's see how to use Photoshop's ruler. Click the arrow of the sixth icon in the **Tools** panel, the dropper tool, and select **Ruler**.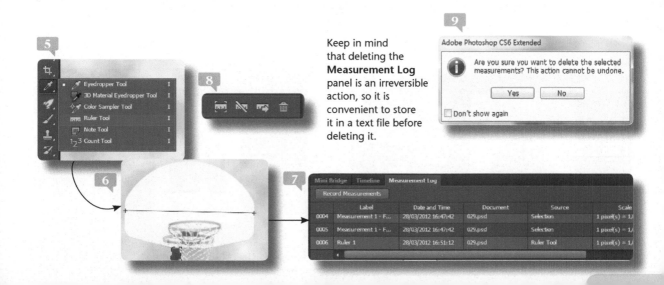

4. This tool is often used to measure angles and linear distances. Create a line by dragging to measure, for example, the width of the backboard. To record this new measurement, press the **Record Measurements** button in the **Measurement Log** panel.

5. The measurement is added to the list. Here's how to save this list in text format .txt. Click the **Select All Measurements**, the first of the icons on the right-hand side of the measurements log.

6. Then click on the third of these icons, which is the **Export selected measurements** icon.

7. The **Save** box opens where you must specify a name and location for the new text file. In the **Name** field enter the term you want. Afterward, select the folder where you want to save the document, then click **Save.**

8. Click the icon showing a trash can in the **Measurements Log** panel to delete the measurements and confirm by pressing the **Yes** button in the box that appears.

9. Finally, press **Ctrl + D** to deselect the image fragment. In the **Ruler** tool bar options, press the **Delete** command to delete the measurement line.

030

IMPORTANT

The data obtained from the measurements are stored in the **Measurement Log** panel, which shares space with the Mini Bridge and Timeline panels, and can be viewed from the Window menu. The measurement log data can be exported to a text file.

Keep in mind that deleting the **Measurement Log** panel is an irreversible action, so it is convenient to store it in a text file before deleting it.

Adobe Photoshop CS6 Extended

Are you sure you want to delete the selected measurements? This action cannot be undone.

Yes   No

☐ Don't show again

Understanding how to work with layers

LAYERS COULD BE DEFINED as different levels with elements that, when brought together, form an entire image or file. This allows you to bring together a large number of individual images and objects in a single document. Generally, the documents that consist of layers always have a background layer that can be created by the user or Photoshop. We can stack as many layers as necessary, and they can be controlled through the Layers panel.

1. To begin to understand the usefulness of the layers system in Photoshop, you will practice with image **031.jpg** which, as always, you can download from our website and save to your Pictures folder. (Of course you can use another similar image, preferably one with a uniform background, if desired). Once you have the file, open it in Photoshop. In the **Layers** panel, which is located on the bottom right of the program window, notice that the image is opened showing it as a background layer (the **Background**). Version CS6 of Photoshop has added a number of functions in the layers pane, which is located at the bottom of the tabs in the panel group, which we will describe throughout this and the following lessons. Next you will need to isolate the subject from the background and insert it in a new document. Before you do this, set a magnification of **80%** by inserting that value in the appropriate field on the **Status** Bar.

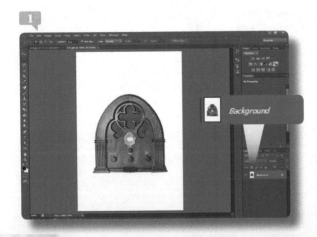

031

2. Now, click the **Magic Wand Tool** in the **Tools** panel and, after establishing a tolerance of **50** and after selecting the **Contiguous** option in **the Options Bar,** click anywhere in the background.

3. With this action, if the background is a solid color, you will have selected the background, not the object. To select the object, open the **Select** menu and click the **Invert** command.

4. With the object selected, open the **Edit** menu and click on the **Copy** option to copy to the clipboard.

5. Press the key combination **Ctrl + N** and in the **New** box, choose **White** as the background content and press **OK**.

6. Pull down the **Edit** menu and click on the **Paste** option.

7. The new document has two layers: the background layer **(Background)** and Layer 1 **(Layer 1)**, which contains the pasted object. The new feature bar is enabled to include more than one layer. Its main function is to quickly locate specific layers by applying filters: imported image layers, adjustment, text, shapes, smart objects, or color. The field that shows by default allows you to visualize the layers containing certain parameters: name, effect, blending mode, or color attributes. Depending on the option chosen in this field, a drop-down box with serveral different options will appear to the right. Complete this exercise by saving the document.

IMPORTANT

The last of the icons in the new functions bar included in the **Layers** panel enables and disables the filters applied to this panel.

7

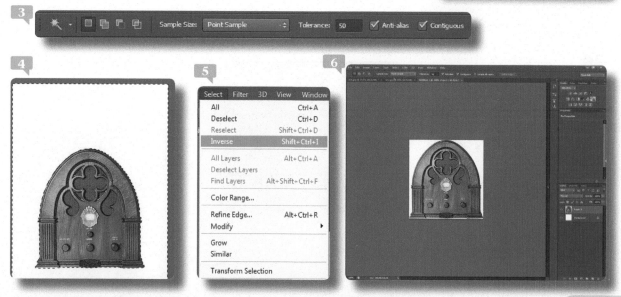

Renaming and locking layers

PHOTOSHOP ALLOWS YOU TO USE an unlimited number of layers in a file. By default, each time you create a layer, the program assigns the layer name and a serial number. Therefore, we recommend renaming the layers with words that identify their contents to faciliate finding the layers that need retouching quickly. All elements of one layer may be positioned anywhere on the canvas unless they have been locked. There are different types of locking in Photoshop: preventing the displacement of an object, that is useful for layers intended for the background, and one that is applied to transparent pixels or applied to the image pixels or its position.

1. In this exercise you will learn how to rename a layer, change its location on the working canvas, and lock it if you do not want it to be modified by mistake. To do this, you will continue to practice with the file created in the previous exercise. First, rename the layer. By default, the program has named it **Layer 1** (remember that the other layer is called by default **Background**).  In the **Layers** pane, double-click the name **Layer 1**.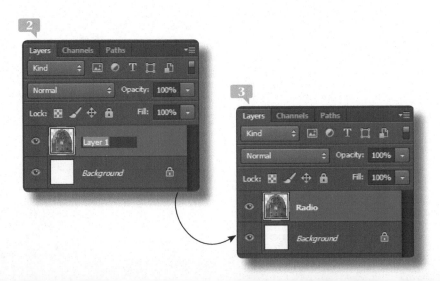

2. Next, type the new name for the layer and press **Return** to confirm.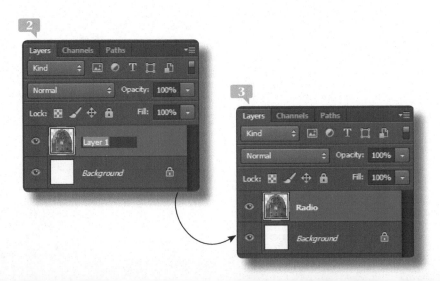

The appearance order of the layers in the **Layers** panel is the stacking order of the different elements of an image.

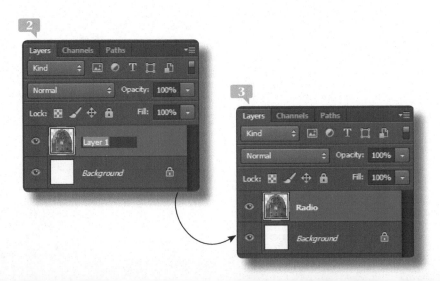

032

3. Now you have your first layer properly identified. Then use the **Move** Tool to move to another location on the canvas—the only object you have at our disposal. Click on this tool, which is the first icon in the **Tools** panel.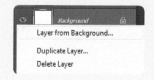

4. Click on the image, hold the mouse button, then drag it to the new point.

5. Now look at the **Lock** Tool. Look for a moment at the background layer. To the right of the name you can see a padlock, indicating that this layer is locked and cannot be changed. Apply the lock feature to the re-named layer and then deactivate it. Click the **Lock All** icon, represented by a drawing of a padlock at the top of the Layers panel.

6. Note that now, next to the name of the layer, you can also see the lock indicator. Taking advantage of the still active **Move Tool**, now try to move the layer.

7. The program launches a dialog box that indicates that it is impossible to perform this action. Click on the **OK** button to accept this.

8. To finish the exercise, unlock this layer. Click on the **Lock All** icon in the **Layers** panel.

IMPORTANT

To change the stacking order, blending mode, or opacity of a background layer it should be converted to a regular layer using the **Layer from Background** option in the context menu.

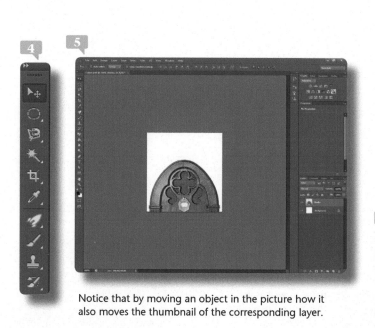

Notice that by moving an object in the picture how it also moves the thumbnail of the corresponding layer.

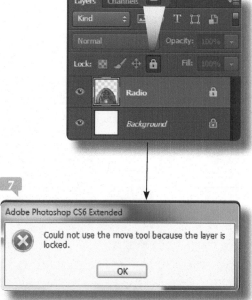

Duplicating and rearranging layers

PHOTOSHOP CAN DOUBLE LAYERS within a document with the option Duplicate Layer, which makes a copy of a layer with its content in accordance with all the original parameters: position and color as well as effects. The duplicate layer can be treated independently. Do not confuse the duplication of layers with the duplication of images. When you duplicate an image, it is located in a new layer, but some of the original parameters such as position are retained.

1. Your objective here is to create an identical layer from the one you created in the previous exercise. You will then apply a series of color characteristics so that it acquires the appearance of a shadow. Make sure that the layer is selected in the **Layers** panel, pull down the **Layer** menu and choose **Duplicate Layer.** 🔲

2. The **Duplicate Layer** Dialog box opens. In the **As** field, type the word **Shade** to specify the new name of the duplicate layer and click **OK**. 🔲

3. Notice that in the **Layers** panel the new layer with the specified name appears. 🔲 In the canvas, you cannot see the new layer because it is hidden behind the original image layer.

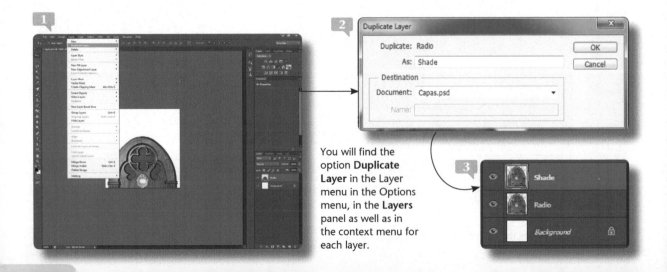

You will find the option **Duplicate Layer** in the Layer menu in the Options menu, in the **Layers** panel as well as in the context menu for each layer.

Let's move the object containing the new layer so you can see it. With the **Move** Tool selected in the **Tools** panel, click on the image and drag it to another location on the canvas.

4. Now it is possible to see the two elements of the layers. Since, as mentioned previously, you use the element of the new layer to create a shadow effect, first, reorganize the layers in the palette, so the **Shade** layer is below the other layer. In the **Layers** panel, click on the **Shade** layer and, without releasing the mouse button, drag it to place it between the renamed layer and the **Background** layer.

5. Adjust the brightness and contrast of the image so that it takes on the appearance of a shadow. In the **Adjustments** pane, click the first icon, the option for **Brightness/Contrast**.

6. Remove the image brightness, and increase the contrast. In the **Brightness** field, type the value −150 and in the **Contrast** field, type the value **80**.

7. Observe the result on the image. Before closing, and to increase the appearance of the shadow, again modify the status of the image relative to the renamed layer. Activate the **Shade** layer by clicking on the image and dragging it into place so as to perfectly simulate a shadow.

IMPORTANT

The reorganization of layers in the **Layers** panel is also very interesting as it allows you to override some images while respecting all its parameters.

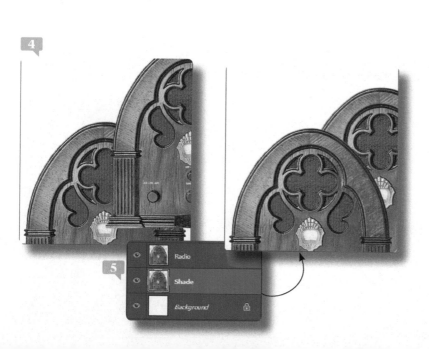

Aligning layers automatically

AUTOMATICALLY ALIGNING LAYERS make the composition of the image more accurate. This Edit menu command quickly analyzes details and moves, or warps, layers to align them perfectly. With this tool, Photoshop aligns layers based on the similarity of their content, allowing you to combine images in different ways: by replacing or removing parts that have the same background, combining images whose content delete or converting video frames to layers to either add or delete content.

1. Use the menu path **File / Scripts / Load Files into Stack** 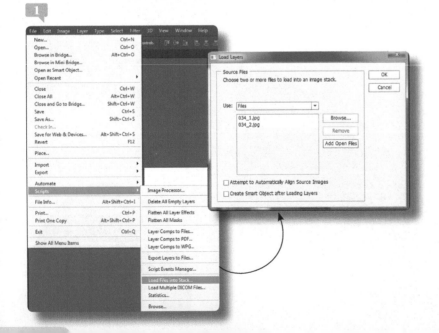 to open in the same document on separate layers the two images with similar content. (You can use the sample images **034_1.jpg** and **034_2.jpg**, which you can find in the download area of our website).

2. Then by using the **Move** tool, move the image of the first layer that is not centered on the canvas.

3. Now select the two layers to line them up. To select adjacent layers, press **Shift + click** on the tabs. Selecting non-adjacent

034

layers is done by using the Ctrl key and click the desired tabs. Click on the second layer by holding down the **Shift** key. Both layers are automatically selected.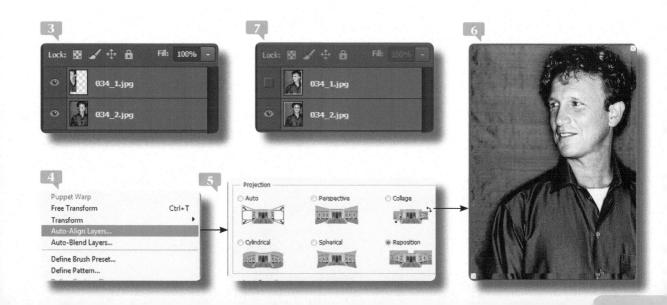

4. Pull down the **Edit** menu and click the **Auto-Align Layers** option.

5. This opens the **Auto-Align Layers** box, where you can choose from six different alignment options: **Automatic, Perspective, Colage, Cylindrical, Spherical** and **Reposition**. Select Reposition, and to proceed with the alignment, press the **OK** button.

6. The two layers are aligned automatically according to content so that they was overlapped equally. Temporarily hide the first layer by clicking on the eye that appears to the left of its name.

7. Both images are correctly aligned. Return the visibility of the layer by clicking on the corresponding box.

8. To finish this simple exercise, pull down the **File** menu, click **Save As** and save the document.

IMPORTANT

Using automatic layer alignment, you can use one of the layers as a reference. Alternatively you can let Photoshop itself choose. In this case, it almost always analyzes all layers, and selects the one at the central position of the resulting composition.

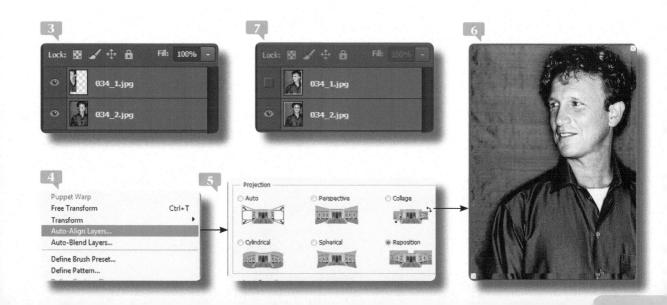

Creating groups of layers

IMPORTANT

In the **Script** command from the **File** menu you will find the tools to export layer comps to separate files, a PDF file, or a web photo gallery.

Layer Comps to Files...
Layer Comps to PDF...
Layer Comps to WPG...

A SET OF LAYERS CAN BE FORMED by layers that may be considered to have common elements relating to a specific image, which can be treated as its own separate group. A set of empty layers is created by supplementing it with the layers you want to group together. You can add layers to a group by dragging them to it, should they already exist, or they can be created directly inside the group.

1. To perform this exercise you should work with an image composed of several layers, like the the file **035.psd** which can be found on our website and saved in your images folder. Select **Layer 7** from the **Layers** panel, click the Options button and choose **New Group.** 1

2. The **New group** box appears, which can also be accessed from the option **New/Group** in the **Layer** menu. The first thing to do is assign the group a distinctive name. In the **Name** field, type the name you want, we suggest product. Given that the group will contain cans of the product from the advert. 2

3. In addition to assigning a name to identify the created group and its component layers, you can also specify a color. Click the arrow button in the **Color** field, select, for example, **Blue** and click **OK.** 3

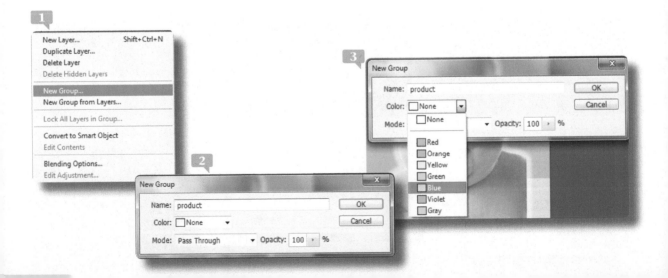

4. Note that above the selected layer appears a folder with the name you created that, at the moment, is empty. To add layers to the created group you must drag them there. In this example, add **7**, **6**, **5**, and **3** to the layer group.

5. The advantage of bringing together multiple layers in a set is that it saves space and provides an overview of the elements that form the composition, while simplifying the management of documents with multiple layers. Click on the arrow preceding the name of the layer set to contract it. Expand it again by pressing the same arrow.

6. You can also create layer groups by selecting them in the **Layers** panel and by using the **Group layers** option from the **Layer** menu. You can also ungroup layers from that menu. You can also create compositions of the layers, which are like snapshots of the state of the **Layers** panel and are used by designers to show their progress to customers. Open the **Window** menu and choose **Layer Comps.**

7. To obtain a composition that reflects the current state of the Layers panel, click on the **Create New Layer Comp,** the fourth icon on the bottom of the panel.

8. The **New Layer Comp** box opens where you can assign a name to the composition, add descriptive comments, and indicate whether to apply the layer's parameters: visibility, position, and appearance. In the **Name** field enter a test name and click **OK.**

9. To close the **Layer Comps** panel click the options button and choose **Close Tab Group.**

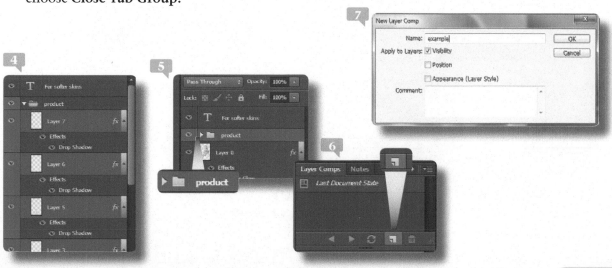

Adjusting opacity to hide layers

TO HIDE ITEMS in a layer, we can use the corresponding visibility box, which is represented by the drawing of an eye in the Layers panel. However, another popular choice for managing the visibility of layers is to change their degree of opacity. Through the Opacity field we can manipulate the percentage of a layer's visibility, a very useful action in case you want to manipulate elements of lower layers without losing reference to the layers above, or to create photomontages.

1. In the **Layers** panel, select, for example, the first layer of the current image, which is the text. **1**

2. Then double-click the **Opacity** field, enter the value **45** and press **Return.** **2**

3. Now the text of the semitransparent layer is chosen so that it blends with the color of the background layer. **3** To recover 100% opacity of this layer, press the arrow and drag that field to the far right of the regulator. **4**

By default, layers have an Opacity of 100%.

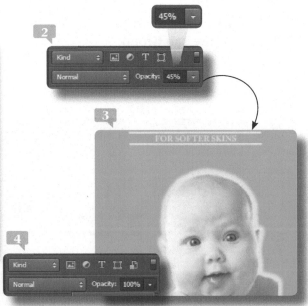

036

4. Next, create a color effect on the sample image by first adding a layer of solid color fill and then modifying its opacity. With the text layer still selected in the **Layers** panel, click the fourth icon on the bottom panel, corresponding to the **Create new fill or adjustment layer,** and from the options that appears, choose **Solid Color.**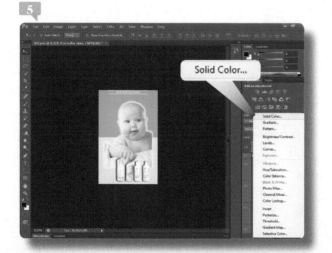

5. This automatically adds a new layer fill with the selected foreground color in the **Tools** panel, while opening the **Color Picker (Solid Color)** box. Select a shade of **orange** in this box and press the **OK** button.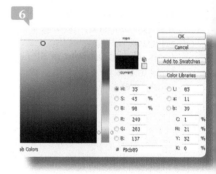

6. Since the new color fill layer is first and has a 100% opacity, it hides the other layers. Click the arrow button in the **Opacity** field in the **Layers** panel and drag the value to **30%.**

7. See the effect. Obviously, depending on the location of the layer, the results will be different. Check what happens when you put the color fill layer between **Layer 0** and **Layer 1.**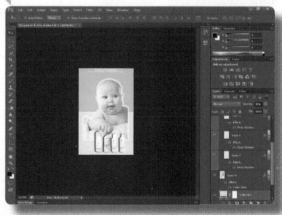

8. You can achieve the same effect as a layer of solid color filled layer, creating a normal layer and painting it with the **Paint Bucket** tool. To finish this exercise, where you have seen the importance of the **Opacity** command in the **Layers** panel, save the resulting image using **Save** from the **File** menu.

Creating fill and adjustment layers

FILL AND ADJUSTMENT LAYERS allow you to apply all necessary changes of light and color without changing the original pixels of an image. Photoshop lets you create three types of fill layers: solid fill color, gradient, or default. These layers can be superimposed on other layers, which can have the effect of obtaining certain optical illusions.

1. To perform this exercise you can use the example image **037.jpg** which is found in the download area of our website. Once you have copied and saved it to your images folder, open it in Photoshop, pull down the **Layer** menu, click on the option **New Fill Layer** and choose **Solid Color.**

2. In the **New Layer** dialog box you can specify a name that identifies the fill layer and select a color to distinguish it from other layers. Click on the arrow button in the **Color** field and choose, for example, Green.

3. To make sure that the fill layer is not completely opaque, double-click the **Opacity** field, and enter a value of **68** and then press **OK**.

4. The layer is created and the **Color Picker (Solid Color)** box appears. In it, select the color you want to fill the new layer and press **OK.**

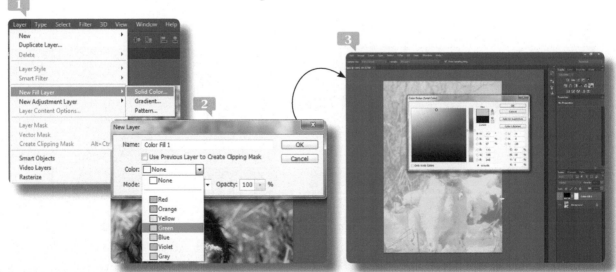

037

5. Then add a new layer over the fill to get a different lighting effect. 🔲 This time, click on the icon showing scales in the **Adjustments** panel to create an adjustment layer for the color balance.

6. Play with the tones and color values of the properties panel to get the right shade.

7. In the second part of this exercise, create a new fill layer, this time using the gradient option. Instead of removing the fill layers and adjustment created, hide them in the **Layers** panel.

8. Open the **Layer** menu, click the **New Fill Layer** command, choose **Gradient** and press the **OK** button in the **New Layer** box.

9. In the **Gradient Fill** box, click on the **Gradient** field 🔲 to open the **Gradient Editor,** select one of the presets and press **OK.** 🔲

10. Back in the **Gradient Fill** box, adjust the different settings depending on the chosen gradient mode, and when happy with the result, click **OK.** 🔲

11. Finally, convert the content of the fill layer to a rasterized layer Open the **Layer** menu, select the **Rasterize** command and click on the **Fill Content** option.

Observe the **Layers** panel as you add fill layers.

Managing fill layers using filters

PHOTOSHOP LETS YOU CREATE AN UNLIMITED NUMBER of fill layers. In the CS6 version of the program, the Layers panel offers new tools to filter and display only only those that interest us in the panel. The available filters are: Filter Pixel Layers, showing the layers with imported images; Filter Adjustment Layers, showing the adjustment layers; Filter Layers of Types, which displays the text layers; Shape Layers Filter, showing the layers containing basic shapes such as ellipses, rectangles or other shapes, and Filter for Smart Objects, which shows the layers that contain smart objects.

1. Click on the **Create new fill or adjustment layer,** which is represented by a black and white circle in the **Layers** panel, and select the **Selective Color** option. [1]
2. Check that there is a new fill layer in the **Layers** panel and that in the **Properties** panel there is the selective color options that allow four-color changes to the amount of each of the primary color components of an image. Press the arrow on the **Colors** field and choose **Whites.** [2]
3. Set the new parameters for the selected color in the fields **Cyan, Magenta, Yellow,** and **Black** so that white is displayed with a blue tone. [3]

IMPORTANT

If you have already created a fill layer in the image, you can create an associated layer so that it can act as a mask by using the techniques you have seen so far. Masks regulate the characteristics of an associated image in detail, so it is advisable to first create a filling layer, which will regulate the intensity of color and the fill color.

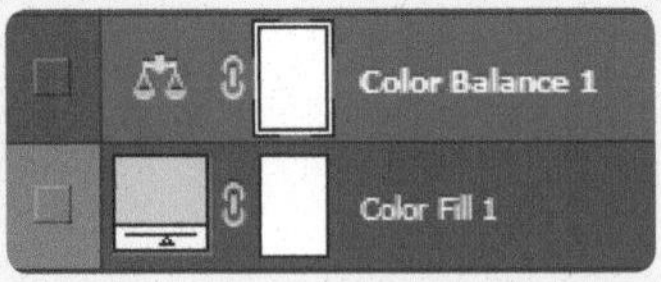

1

2

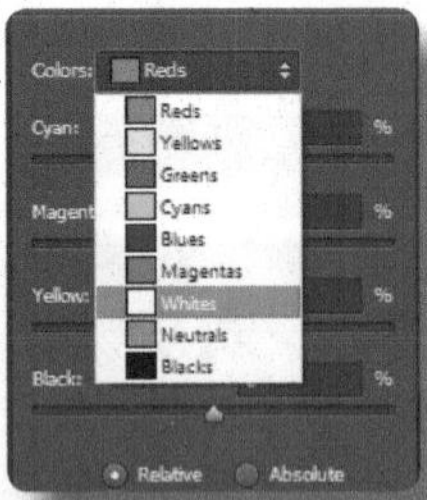

3

4. Before starting the filter layer, you will add another fill layer. Click on the **Create new fill or adjustment layer** and this time choose the option **Brightness/Contrast.**

5. Adjust the brightness and contrast in the properties panel.

6. Once carried out these actions you will have several fill layers. 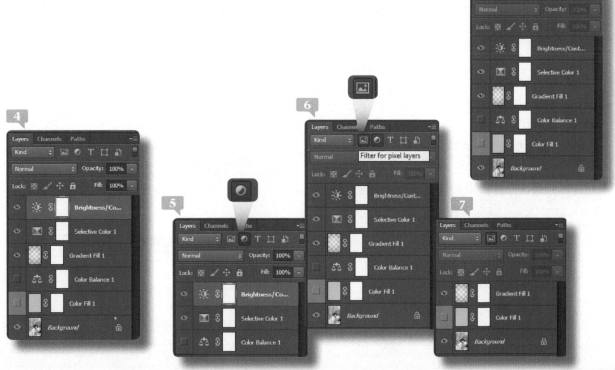 Now imagine that your document has many more that you can't see just with a simple look. In these cases filtering the layers is more useful. In the new filter bar in the Layers panel, located, as you know, under the tabs of the panel group, click on the second icon, which shows a circle of two colors and is called **Filter for adjustment layers.**

7. See what has happened: only the layers that correspond to the adjustment are shown in the layers panel. The three fills created in this and the previous exercise. Remeber that you can activate both filters for different layers. Check it by clicking the filter icon to the left of the active **Filter for pixel layers.**

8. They are added to existing layers that meet the requirements of the selected filter. Clear the filter adjustment layers by clicking on it again.

9. Finally, click on the icon at the right end of the filter bar to disable any active filter.

Adding fill layers with patterns

REPETITIVE PATTERNS CAN BE USED to fill areas of an image. The characteristics of the selected pattern used to form a fill layer can be manipulated from the Pattern Fill box, which can increase or reduce the scale, link to the layer, or adjust the source.

1. We recommend using an image with a uniform background as in image **039.jpeg**, which you can download from our website. Select the **Magic Wand Tool** and click on the background of the image to select it.

2. Click on the **Create new fill or adjustment layer,** the fourth icon at the bottom of the **Layers** panel, and from the drop-down menu, select the **Pattern** option.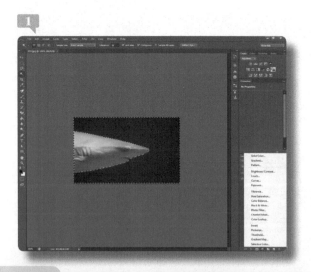

3. The **Pattern Fill** box appears, while the first applied pattern is applied to the base of the image. Click the arrow button in the sample and click on the icon that looks like a sun to see the options.

4. You can see that Photoshop classified the categories into different sections based on what you predefined. Select the category **Artist Surfaces** 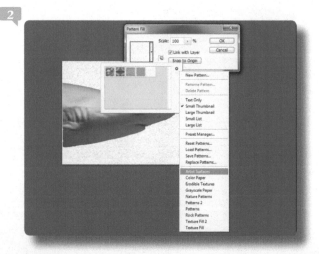 and in the dialog box that appears, click the **Append** button to add, not replace, the existing pattern of the chosen category.

5. Select one of the artistic motifs and, before clicking **OK**, increase the value of the scale to **200**.

6. In the **Layers** panel, check that the pattern has been placed above the background layer and affects only the selected pixels. Double-click the **Opacity** field, enter the value **50** and press **Return**.

7. To continue the exercise, hide the adjustment layer.

8. Photoshop lets you use your own pictures to create patterns. Open the program work area from the image, which will create the pattern (use the example image **039_01.jpg**).

9. You will turn an image into a pattern. Pull down the **Edit** menu and choose **Define Pattern**.

10. In the **Pattern Name** box is a thumbnail of the pattern you are about to create. By default, the program identifies the new pattern with the name of the source file. Click **OK** to complete the action.

11. Select the first image, select the background again with the Magic Wand, click **Create new fill or adjustment layer** and choose **Pattern**.

12. The pattern created from the image already appears in the **Pattern Fill** box ready to be applied. Set a scale of **180%** and click **OK** to apply.

IMPORTANT

To display the default library of patterns use the **Reset Patterns** in the pop-up menu in the patterns palette.

> Reset Patterns...
> Load Patterns...
> Save Patterns...

Transforming, rotating, and flipping layers

> **IMPORTANT**
>
> When using the **Free Transform** Tool, hold down the Shift key while dragging the corner handle, to get 15 degree turns.

THERE ARE DIFFERENT WAYS TO TRANSFORM an image in a layer, the most common is by dragging the markers of the defined rectangle with the Free Transform, Scale, Skew, Distortion, or Perspective tools. Another approach is to modify the values of the Options Bar according to the chosen tool. Photoshop can also rotate and flip the image in a layer.

1. To perform this exercise, you can use, if you want, document **040.psd** which can be found on our website. To resize the image in Layer 1, select that layer, open the **Edit** menu and choose **Free Transform.** [1] (If the layer in question is the background layer, you must first convert it to a regular layer using the **Layer from background** option in the context menu.)
2. If using the handles located at the top and bottom, the height of the image is distorted, using the side handles will modifiy the width. To change the image size while maintaining its proportions, it is necessary to drag the handles at the corners of the delineated rectangle while holding down the **Shift** key.

1

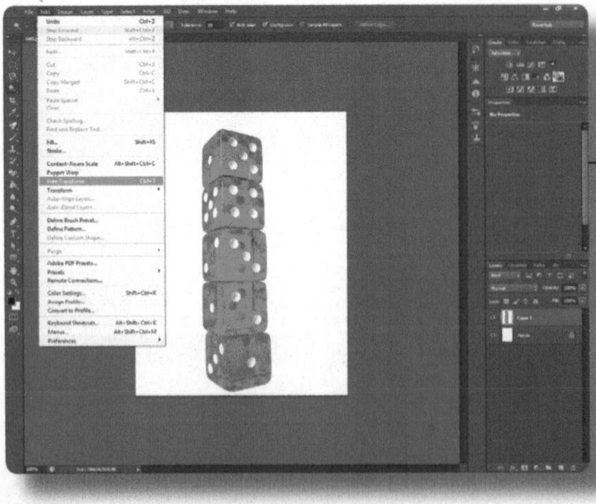

2

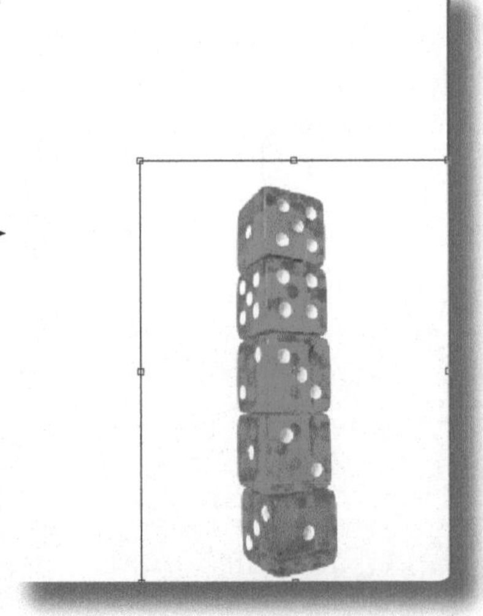

Click the handle at the top left, and holding this key down, drag to get a smaller size.

3. The **Free Transform Tool** also lets you change the image position in the document. Click on the selected image and drag it into place in the center of the canvas.

4. To apply the changes to the current file, click the **Commit Transform** icon showing as a check mark in the far right of the **Options Bar** or press the **Return** key.

5. Now you will modify the size of the image but this time using the **Options Bar**. Open the **Edit** menu, click **Transform** and select **Scale**.

6. Enter the value **50** in the W field of the Options Bar, referring to the width, then type the same value in the area regarding height, H, and press **Return**.

7. Open the **Edit** menu, click the **Transform** command and choose **Flip Horizontal**.

8. Pull down the **Edit** menu, click on the **Transform** command and select **Rotate 90° CCW**.

9. Finally, turn the image by setting the rotation angle and direction. Open the **Edit** menu, click on the **Free Transform** option, enter the value **45** in the **Angle** field in the Options Bar and press **Return** twice.

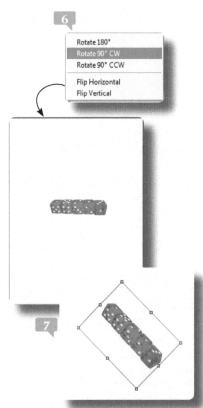

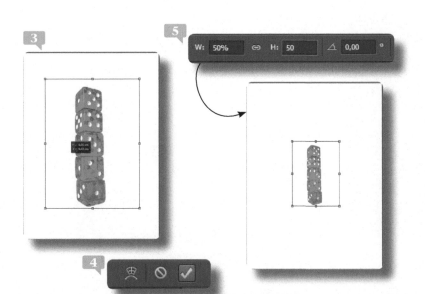

Deforming the content of an image

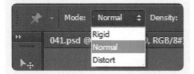
THE PUPPET WARP TOOL ALLOWS THE RADICAL transformation of specific areas of an image while others are anchored in place. When you activate this tool, Photoshop provides a visual screen that can distort the image areas, which is especially useful for retouching the form of hair or changing the position of arms and legs, for example.

1. In this exercise you will practice with the sample file **041.psd**, which you can download from our website and store in the images folder. The file is composed of two layers, one with a white background color, and the other with a transparent background, which houses the object you are going to warp. To begin, select this layer in the **Layers** panel. 📭

2. Open the **Edit** menu and choose **Puppet Warp**. 🔁

3. Notice that the object you will warp now appears on the screen. 🔁 Keep in mind that if the layer of the object has a transparent background, make sure the mesh doesn't cover the background. If not, the warp will affect the object differ-

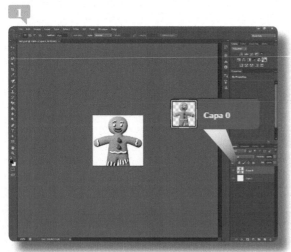

So that the mesh covers only the object to be processed, it must be placed on a transparent background layer.

041

ently. Suppose you want to move the left arm up without affecting the rest of the object. Insert several points on the head, body, and right arm to establish them as fixed points. (Note that the more fixed points created, the more realistic the effect).

4. Then click the left end of the arm and, without releasing the mouse button, drag that point up.

5. Simple, right? The arm is moved upward without the rest of the object being affected by the warp. You will also move the right arm. To do this, you must first remove the fixed locations of the arm. Click on each of them with the right mouse button and choose **Delete Pin.**

6. Keep the rest of the fixed locations, and create a new location at the right end of the arm and drag it up.

7. Remember that if you position the pointer near a location while holding the **Alt** key down, you can rotate the screen by dragging it around. We suggest you continue to give movement to this item on your own to realize the enormous potential of this tool. Once you have warped the cookie, click the **Commit Puppet Warp** icon, which appears as a check mark in the far right of the **Options Bar,** and save the changes if the result pleases you. Finish the exercise by closing the image.

The visual aids provided by Photoshop CS6 to perform the basic processing actions allow you to control precise movements.

Inserting and editing text

TEXT IS INCLUDED IN A SINGLE LAYER and is treated independently from other objects. From the Character panel we can modify any parameters or characteristics of the text, while the Paragraph panel has the necessary options to align text, add a specific indentation, or increase the space before or after the paragraph.

1. To perform this exercise you can use any picture you like. To start, in the **Tools** panel, click the **Horizontal Type Tool**, whose icon shows a T. 📕

2. To enter text in the image, click anywhere on the canvas and type a word. 🔲

3. To insert text press **Commit any current edit** in the **Options Bar.**

4. When you start entering text in the **Layers** panel there is a new layer, which has adopted the name of the text inserted in it, and shows an icon with the letter T indicating that this is a text layer. By default, Photoshop has activated a specific font and size. After inserting the text, you can resize it. Double click on the word to select it in the **Options Bar,** click the ar-

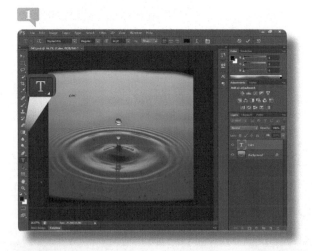

row buttonin the **Set font size** field, and choose, for example, the value **36**.

042

5. To reposition the text, select the **Move Tool** in the **Tools** panel and drag the text to the desired location.

6. Now open the **Window** menu and select **Character.**

7. You will reduce the horizontal scale of the letters. In the **Character** panel, the **Horizontal Scale** field is headed by the letter T on a double horizontal arrow. Double-click on that field, type, for example, the value **75** and press **Return.**

8. To apply an underlining effect, in the **Character** panel, click on the highlighted command, which displays an underlined T.

9. Then, click the **Paragraph** tab and verify that this panel shows the settings required to change the alignment; indents; left, right, and front-line space before and after the paragraph, as well as automatic hyphenation.

10. Click again on the **Character** tab, click the arrow button **Set the anti-aliasing method** field, located at the bottom right of the panel, and select **Strong.**

11. Click on **Set font-family**, the first item in the **Character** panel, and select the font you want.

12. To conclude the exercise, click the Options button of the pane and choose **Close Tab group**.

Smoothing makes the edges of the text smooth by partially filling the edge pixels so that they merge with the background.

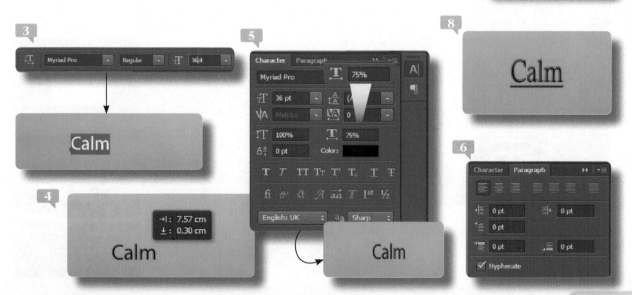

Creating and editing text masks

MASKS ALLOW YOU to insert text, which then becomes a selection area that can be moved, copied, filled, and contoured like any other selection. To do this, Photoshop offers a Horizontal Mask Type Tool and one for vertical text. These are very useful, for example, when creating text with a fill image —the overlay of text on an image. If desired, a mask can have the effect of a shadow or stroke type applied to it.

1. In the following example you will use file **043.psd,** which as always, you can find in the download area of our website. To begin, click the arrowhead of the **Horizontal Type**, select the **Horizontal Type Mask Tool** 🖳 and click on the bottom of the image.

2. It automatically displays a red screen that covers the entire document. 🔲 This indicates that everything from now on will be considered a mask. Type a sample word and then select it by double clicking on it.

3. From the **Options Bar**, increase the size to about 120 and confirm the change from the same bar. 🔳

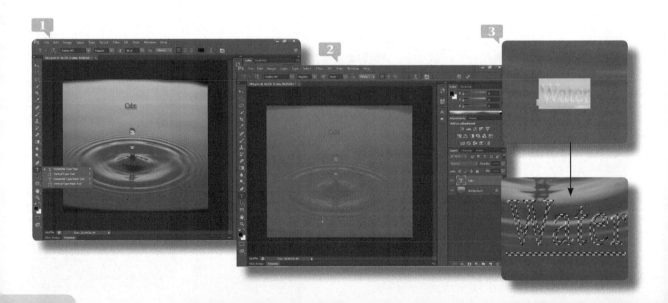

043

4. When approving the changes, the red layer disappears and the text is displayed as the selection area. This selection area allows you to copy and paste the space that was occupied to create objects with the bottom of the text just below the selection. Let's try it. Make sure that the background layer is selected, open the **Edit** menu, click on the **Copy** option and create a new document from the **File** menu.

5. If the selected layer is the one with the text of the document, using the **Copy** command will generate a dialog box that indicates the impossability of copying the contents because the layer is empty. Open the **Edit** menu, click on the **Paste Special** option and choose **Paste in Place.**

6. Depending on the size of the source document and the target, you may have to reduce the size of the new layer using the **Free Transform Tool** you already know, or simply move it with the **Move Tool.** You will now apply an effect to the layer to highlight it. In the **Layers** panel, click the Options button and choose **Blending Options.**

7. In the **Layer Style** box, click the **Stroke** option.

8. This style allows you to create a colored fringe around the selected object. In the **Size** field enter the value **5** and apply the selected style by pressing **OK.**

9. It is interesting to see how the fusion effects are represented on the text layer in the Layers panel. Save the new document with the name you want, then close it.

Distorting text

THE WARP TEXT TOOL lets you apply preset distortions to any text, regardless of their size and initial appearance. The relationship of text distortion is concentrated in the Warp Text box, which besides allowing the selection of up to fifteen different styles of distortion, it allows you to modify parameters in the Bend, Horizontal Distortion, and Vertical Distortion fields. After you apply a style of distortion you can modify the text as if it were the original.

1. In the **Layers** panel, click on the layer containing the text to distort and select it. [1]

2. Click the arrowhead of the **Horizontal Type Mask Tool** and select the **Horizontal Type Tool.** [2]

3. Once you activate the text tool, click on the word to be distorted. [3]

4. Then, in the **Options Bar,** click the **Create warped text** icon, represented by the letter T with a curved line below it. [4]

5. The **Warp Text** box opens. There you must choose one of the fifteen existing types, which are shown in the sample chart

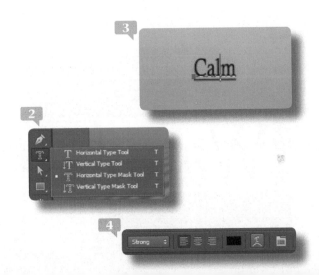

that accompanies each one. Pull down the **Style** menu box and choose the type of distortion as **Arc**.

6. By selecting any distortion, it activates three sliders to modify the curve, the horizontal or vertical distortion. Double-click the field **Bend** and insert the value **–10** so that the curve is generated toward the opposite side.

7. Double-click the field **Vertical Distortion** and insert the value **–15**. Then press the **OK** button to apply the effect.

8. Click again on the **Create warped text** in the **Options Bar** to open the **Warp Text** box, open the **Style** field and select, for example, **Wave**.

9. Double-click the field **Bend,** enter the value **–38**, double-click the field **Horizontal Distortion,** enter the value **8** and press the **OK** button.

10. Remember that even if you changed the appearance of text, it is still active without losing its properties, so you can modify, replace, or add new text without losing its shape. Double-click the word to select it, click on the color box in the **Options Bar,** choose a different hue in the **Color Picker (Text Color)** box and press **OK** to apply it.

11. Finish the exercise by confirming the changes from the Options Bar and checking the effect.

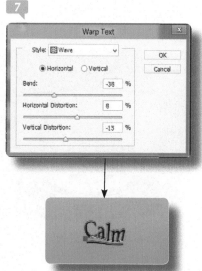

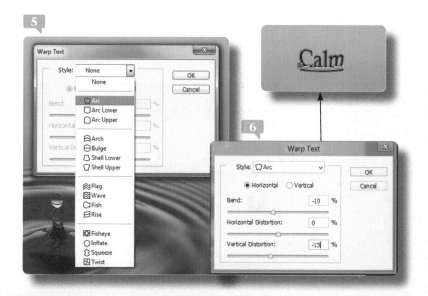

Creating 3D text

ALTHOUGH THE FUNCTIONS FOR CREATING 3D IMAGES and text are not in themselves new, Photoshop CS6 has a spectacular new 3D function. It is an interface to manage the viewpoint and the lighting of the canvas.

1. To begin, select the Horizontal Text Tool in the tool palette and type a word on the image, any word that you want.

2. A new text layer will appear in the **Layers** panel. Change text properties, if desired, according to their preferences from the Options Bar or the **Character** panel.

3. After confirming the insertion of the text, check it in the Options Bar at about the height of the panels is an icon that shows the term in 3D. This icon is the first new one concerning the 3D functions in Photoshop CS6. With the new text layer selected, click on this icon. (If the icon is not mentioned in the interface, pull down the **Text** menu and click on the **Extrude to 3D** command.)

4. A dialog box appears where you indicate that you want to generate a 3D layer and confirm that you want to switch to the new 3D workspace. Click on the **Yes** button and wait a few seconds for the 3D workspace to load.

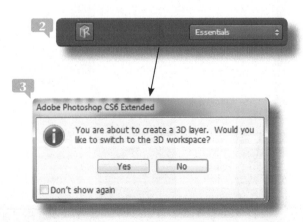

5. In addition to creating the new 3D layer, the image is now in a 3D space that allows full interaction while managing it. The first thing you must check is how 3D text is dealt with. To do this, turn the text 3D rotation tool, enabled by default in the Options Bar, in the **3D Mode** section.

6. Note that the processing power of your computer will determine whether 3D manipulation appears fast or slow. According to the icon enabled in the Options Bar, you can rotate or orbit around the text, move and even change its size. Each of these actions is represented by handles on the text in the image.

7. At the top of the screen you can see a white circle. Click on it and see what happens. 5

8. In the center of the workspace an image of a sphere appears, which is used to indicate the point from which the text should be lighted in 3D. Move the smaller sphere located at the opposite end of the line connecting both areas to direct the light as you want, and when finished, press the white circle to turn off the light. (Note that this icon will have changed position in the image.)

9. To exit the 3D space, select a different layer or a new tool.

IMPORTANT

The panel at the top left of the image to activate a 3D layer allows to preview the image from different angles: from the right, up, down, front, etc.

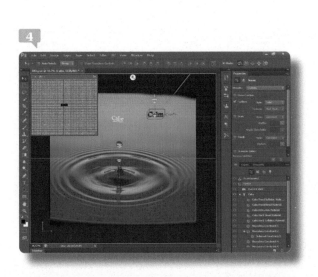

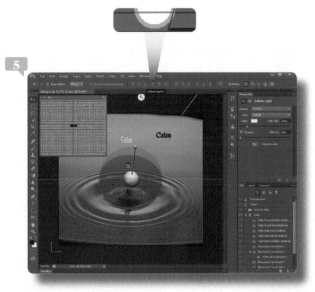

Adding and customizing a drop shadow

LAYER STYLES ARE EFFECTS or treatments that can be applied to custom objects in the layers of a document to add or modify striking effects without changing the content of the original layer. Photoshop has up to ten different types of layer styles, each of which has predefined parameters so you can easily apply them. A layer style that includes the object of an image may be copied and pasted onto other objects in the same image or in another image while maintaining the same characteristics.

1. Download **046.psd** from our website, save it to your images folder. Then open it in Photoshop. Apply a drop shadow effect on the text layer. With that layer selected, open the **Layer** menu, click on the **Layer Style** command and choose **Drop Shadow.** 🔧

2. The display shows the **Layer Style** box, 🔧 which contains the complete list of effects and styles that can be added to the objects in a layer. Since you have already selected the **Drop Shadow**, this is the style that appears on it. Although it is possible to apply the effect with the default parameters, you

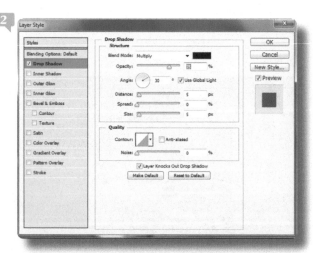

Each layer's styles can be applied to the default layer styles defined by the program or can be customized from the **Layer Style** box.

can also modify any of them to customize our settings. Click the color box at the top of the **Structure** section, next to the **Blend Mode** field.

3. The display opens the familiar dialog box **Color Picker.** Click on a shade of the Vertical Color Bar, choose a color from the color box and press **OK** to apply it.

4. Click on the arrow button in the **Blend Mode** field and select the **Normal** option. ▣

5. Double-click the **Angle** field and type, for example, the value **100.**

6. Then also change the distance between the object and shadow. In the **Distance** field, enter the value **10.**

7. By doing this, you have established a distance of 10 pixels between the object and its shadow. The **Spread** value is equal to the thickness of the shadow. Type in this field, for example, the value **20** and, in the **Size** field, insert the value **7.** ▣

8. Finally, apply a new outline style. Click the arrow button on the **Contour** field and select one of the styles available. ▣

9. To conclude the exercise, modify slightly the opacity of the shadow. In the **Opacity** field, enter the value **50** and apply the new settings by pressing **OK.** ▣

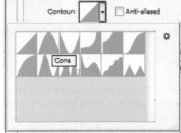

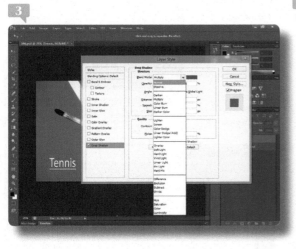

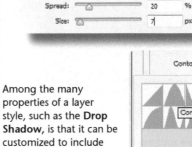

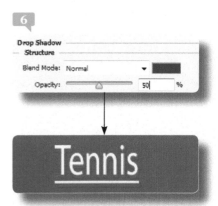

Among the many properties of a layer style, such as the **Drop Shadow**, is that it can be customized to include opacity, the distance between the object and shadow, outline, etc.

Applying bevels and embossing text

ONE OF THE MOST USED LAYER STYLES for compositions created in Photoshop, which has the function to highlight a text object, is the layer style Bevel and Emboss. This style allows an outline to be given to a determind object. In the Layer Style dialog box, you can determine the style of the bevel, width, size of the shadow, and the direction or angle of light.

1. Begin by selecting the text layer in the **Layers** pane. ▪ Click the command second from the bottom on this panel, which corresponds to **Add a layer style**, then select the **Bevel & Emboss** style. ▪

2. First modify the style of the bevel. Click on the **Style** field and select **Outer Bevel.** ▪

3. Thanks to the real-time update, you can check the effect of the selected bevel style on the text as it is modified. Now change the style of the bezel, allowing you to define more mild or more pronounced relief of the text. Pull down the **Technique** field and choose **Chisel Hard.** ▪

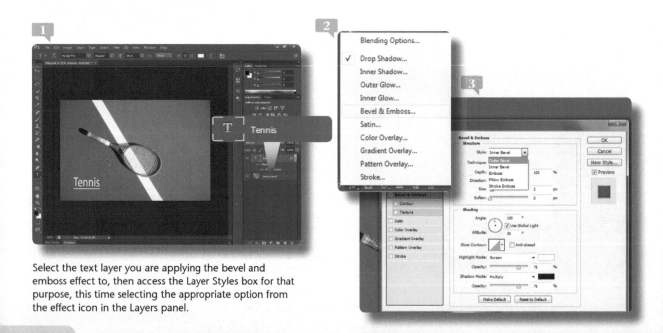

Select the text layer you are applying the bevel and emboss effect to, then access the Layer Styles box for that purpose, this time selecting the appropriate option from the effect icon in the Layers panel.

047

4. Note that the relief is much more evident. Then establish a change of direction for the relief effect. Enable **Down** in the **Direction** command.

5. Also change the size of the bezel. Double-click the **Size** field and insert the value **10**.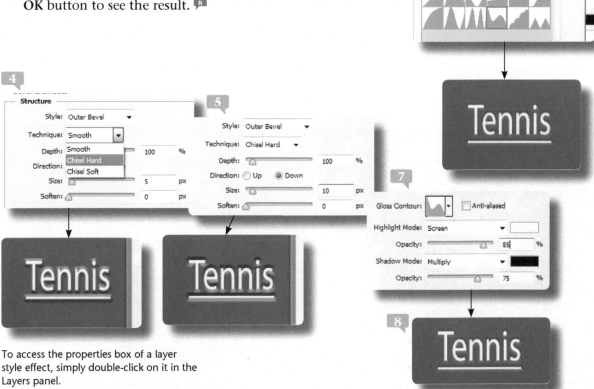

6. The effect is clearly visible. Return to establish a size for a more moderate bevel, so that the relief effect is visible but not so marked. Insert **4** in the **Size** field.

7. Also change the direction of the effect created. Click the **Up** option button in the **Direction** parameter.

8. Reverse the angle of the shadow so that the light direction is contrary to the present value. Double-click the field **Angle** and insert the value **–90**.

9. Finally, select the **Contour** option in the category panel, open the sample **Gloss Contour** option and apply by double-clicking one of the styles available.

10. Check the effect achieved on the text with the new outline parameters. Finally, double-click the **Opacity** field for the **Highlight Mode** settings and enter a value of **85** then press the **OK** button to see the result.

IMPORTANT

While this is a style that is often applied to text objects to highlight them on the other elements of the document, you can also add it to all kinds of images.

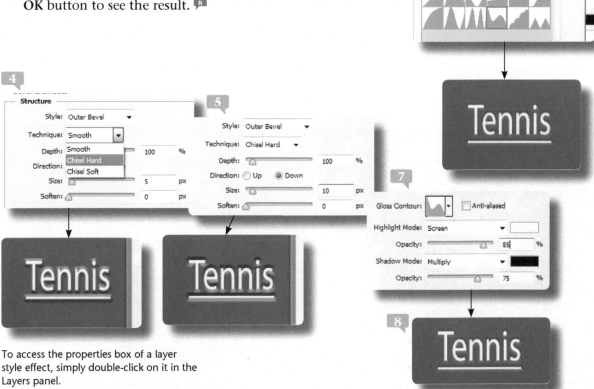

To access the properties box of a layer style effect, simply double-click on it in the Layers panel.

Overlaying colors and gradients

WHEN INSERTING TEXT in Photoshop, you must assign a font, a size, and a color. These characteristics can be modified at any time, but Photoshop has a tool that allows you to perform the same action as a style layer: colors and gradients overlaying.

1. For this exercise, use file **046_1.psd**, an update of **046.psd.** If you prefer, insert a new text layer. Select the **Layers** panel for the text layer **Sports**, click on the icon **Add a layer style**, the second from the bottom of the panel, and select the **Color Overlay** style.

2. The **Layer Style** box shows the characteristics of the chosen style. Click the color swatch next to the **Blend Mode** field to access the **Color Picker** box.

3. Click on the desired color in the vertical color bar then press **OK** to apply.

4. Check the effect on the final text before applying the style. The text object has been colored with the chosen tone.

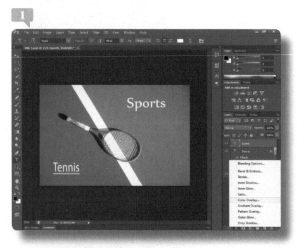

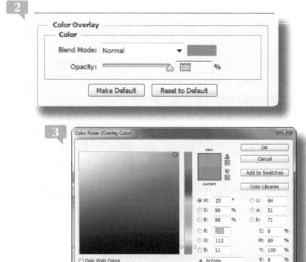

Layer styles Color Overlay, Gradient Overlay, and Pattern Overlay fill the contents of the layer with a color, gradient, or pattern, so the original color is not affected and always remains available.

048

Note that the text has only one color overlay layer that you can remove whenever you need to re-arrange the original color. You will modify some of the options of the applied style. Open the **Blend Mode** menu and choose **Dissolve**.

5. Then double-click the **Opacity** field, enter the value **54** and press **OK** to apply the changes.

6. Apply the **Dissolve** style with an opacity of 54%. Photoshop hasn't applied the color evenly. Here, we show the effect that can be achieved by applying a gradient overlay. Open the Styles panel, click the check box to disable **Color Overlay** and select the **Gradient Overlay** effect.

7. This style allows you to add a gradient layer composed of several colors to the selected text object. The color gradient applied by default is black and white. Display the **Blend Mode** field and select **Hard Light.**

8. This style can allow much more contrast between the different colors that form the gradient. Pull down the menu for the **Gradient** field and choose, for example, the default shown in the colors orange and yellow.

9. Finally, double-click the **Scale** field, type the value **50** and press **OK** to see the effect.

IMPORTANT

The **Color Overlay** style allows the application of a specific color to a text object by increasing or decreasing its strength or blending mode, which allows you to have the original color of the text available. The **Gradient Overlay** style, meanwhile, lets you apply a gradient of colors from both presets and customized ones—in this case, the lattice of color blending mode, the angle of inclination, and the mode which shows the gradient.

Overlaying patterns

THE PATTERN OVERLAY LAYER STYLE acts like the Color Overlay and Gradient Overlay styles, but it is different in that instead of applying one or more colors on a text object or an image, it applies a preset pattern from Photoshop or one which has been created by the user. The patterns may be modified to appear more or less intense. The Overlaying Pattern style can be combined Gradient Overlay, so that the patterns appear graduated as a function of the settings used in the style Gradient Overlay.

1. In this lesson you will add the **Pattern Overlay** layer style to the text object you added the gradient layer to in the previous exercise. To begin with, and with the text layer selected, click on the icon **Add a layer style** from the **Layers** panel, then choose **Pattern Overlay.** 🔲

2. You can apply a preset Photoshop pattern or a pattern created personally as fill content for text or images. 🔲 Click **OK** to display the text object with the default preset pattern.

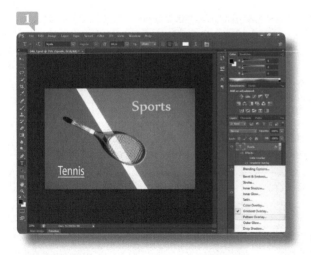

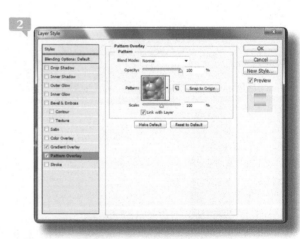

If you want the pattern you choose to move with the layer as it moves, keep **Link with Layer** selected.

049

3. Because the layer has applied the **Gradient Overlay** style, the new layer style seems not to affect the text. For this pattern to appear in full, hide this style. Remember that you can do so by disabling the **Layer Style** box or by clicking the visibility icon in the **Layers** panel. Run this second action to hide it. **3**

4. Now notice the effect. **4** Next, apply another preset. Double-click the **Pattern Overlay** layer in the **Layers** panel.

5. Click the arrow button in the **Pattern** field, click the round arrow button and choose, for example, the option **Patterns. 5**

6. In the dialog box that appears, click the **Append** button so that new patterns are added to those already shown. **6**

7. Scroll through the gallery and select the patterns that you like with a double-click. **7**

8. Now you will apply a new pattern. Open the menu **Pattern** and select another pattern.

9. Before applying the pattern, you should modify its appearance. Double-click the **Scale** field, enter the value **200** and press **OK** to apply the new pattern and to see the result. **8**

8

If you want the source of the pattern the same as the document, select the **Snap to origin**.

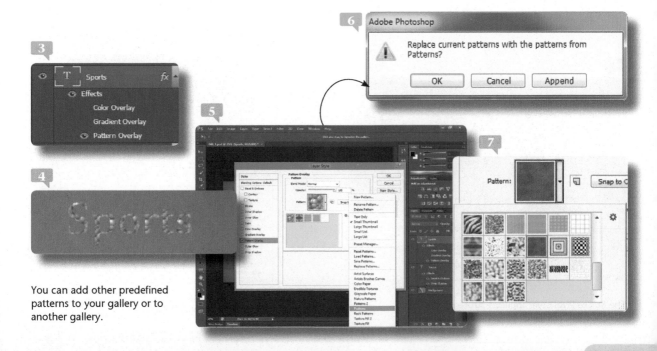

You can add other predefined patterns to your gallery or to another gallery.

Enhancing text with a Stroke style

THE STROKE LAYER STYLE CREATES A BORDER with a certain thickness and color to enhance a text object or an image. The Layer Style box provides the options necessary so the Stroke style can be adapted to the characteristics of each element of your image. The thickness of the edge, which must always be appropriate to the object that it affects is very important, as is the color. In regards to the color, it is advisable to set a different fill color, so that there is an obvious contrast between the two.

1. To begin with, and after making sure that the layer where you are applying the effect is selected, click the **Add a Layer Style** and select **Stroke.** (You can add text to the image **046.psd** as in the example.) [1]

2. The **Layer Style** box shows the characteristics of the **Stroke** style. You can apply a gradient, pattern, or color to the stroke. By default, the solid color chosen for the line is black. [2] Click the color swatch in the **Color** field to display the Color Picker. [3]

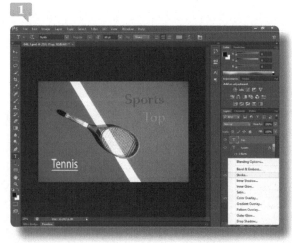

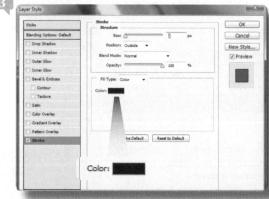

The Stroke layer style applies a stroke to an object using a color, gradient, or pattern.

3. In the Color Picker, choose the color you want and press the **OK** button to apply it. 🔲4

4. As usual, you can view the text changes as you make them. 🔲5 This ensures that the end result will be exactly what you are looking for before applying them for good. Double-click the **Size** field and insert a value of **5** to significantly increase the Stroke weight. 🔲6

5. The Position filed allows you to start the line from a particular point of the text object, from within it, or from outside it, as well as from the center. In this case display the **Position** field and choose **Inside** to verify the change. 🔲7

6. Before applying the changes, you will look at the blending mode, to visualize the effect one way or another depending on the colors and the light available. Click the arrow button of the **Blend Mode** field and select **Vivid Light**. 🔲8

7. You can see that, with this blending mode, the stroke is more enhanced. Click **OK** to apply the new layer style and to end the exercise.

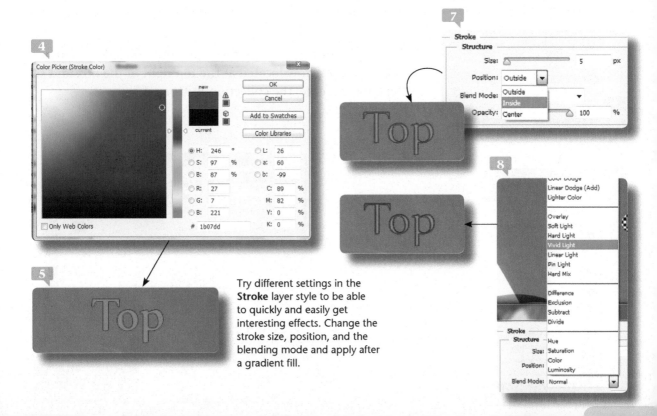

Try different settings in the **Stroke** layer style to be able to quickly and easily get interesting effects. Change the stroke size, position, and the blending mode and apply after a gradient fill.

Using the layer styles collections

PHOTOSHOP HAS A LARGE NUMBER of predefined styles grouped together in the style collections. The default styles can be modified and customized, and saved as a new style. Any default style collection offers a small sample of the effects its elements can produce.

1. Begin by removing the layer of text you worked with in the previous exercise: the **Stroke** layer style in the **Layers** panel, by dragging it to the trash can icon.

2. With the same text layer selected, click the **Add a layer style** from the **Layers** pane, then click the **Blending Options** command.

3. In the dialog box of the **Layer Style** options, click the **Styles** option to view the Photoshop default styles.

4. The default style catalog is shown in the middle of the dialog box. Choose one of the samples and note the appearance of the written word in the layer.

5. The program not only provides just this collection of styles. Click on the arrow located at the top right of the box and select, for example, the collection **Buttons.**

The blending mode of a layer determines how the pixels of that layer are fused with the underlying pixels of the image. You can see the blending options available in the Layer Style box.

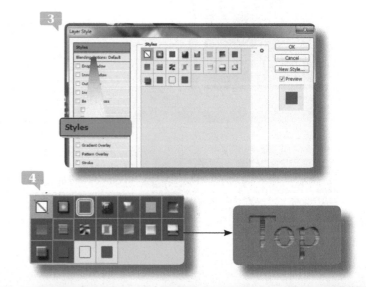

6. Photoshop asks if you want to replace the current collection of styles for the ones you have chosen. Click **OK** to confirm.

7. Click on the style called **Smoke** from the style collection you have loaded.

8. Although all these styles have certain settings, you can modify some of their features. In the **Layer Style** box, click on the **Bevel & Emboss** option to view those settings.

9. Open the **Style** field menu and choose **Emboss.**

10. Modify the size and angle of the relief effect and then apply the changes by clicking **OK.**

11. You can now apply another library layer style on the bottom of the image. Keep in mind that for this to happen you have to first convert the background layer into a normal layer. Select it in the **Layers** panel, click on it with the right mouse button and choose **Layer from Background.** Create a new layer by pressing the **OK** button on the **New Layer** box.

12. Click **Add a Style Layer** and then click the **Blending Options** command.

13. Click the **Styles** category, then click on the button library options and choose the **Image Effects** category.

14. To add these styles to the gallery, click the **Append** button.

15. Now select one of the added styles and click **OK** to apply it to the background. You have now finished the exercise.

051

IMPORTANT

The thumbnail view of the style collections can be modified so that they display the name of the style and a thumbnail, a list of only names, or larger samples.

Creating new layer styles

YOU CAN CREATE NEW LAYER STYLES BASED on existing ones or from scratch, you can then save them to different menus that use preset styles. The simplest method to create a new style is to customize a pre-established style by personalizing the features to achieve the desired result. Once saved, this new style will appear along with the others and may be used in new compositions.

1. To start, we suggest that you create a new text layer with the content you want, where you will apply a custom layer style and then save it with the rest of the preset layer styles. To start with, in the **Layers** panel, select the layer containing the element to which you want to apply the effect.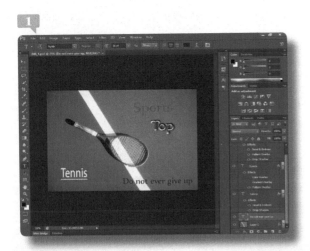

2. Click the **Add a layer style** panel and select the **Blending Options** command.

3. In the **Layer Style** box, click the **Styles** option.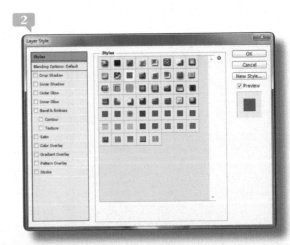

4. The most recently used collection of styles appears. Select one of the styles from the collection, customize some of the

options and save it to the menu as if it were a new style. Click one of the styles to select it.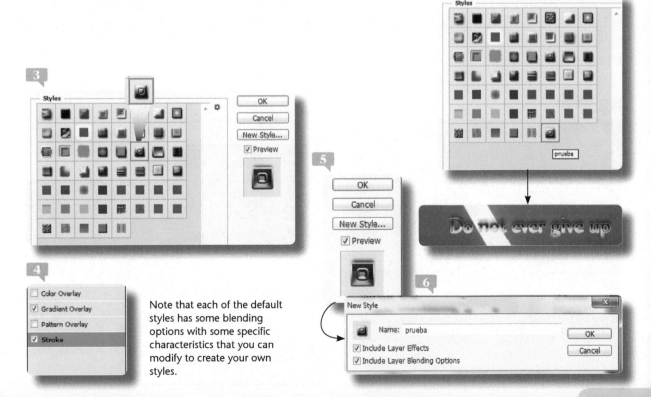

5. Then select one of the effects that the style has to access its settings.

6. Change some of these parameters and look at the achieved effect on the layer (you can do this without applying the changes if the **Preview** option is enabled).

7. Then, save the layer style features you've included, so that you can apply it later to other elements of compositions created with Photoshop. Click the **New Style** button.

8. In the **New Style** dialog box you must specify the name of the new style that, from this moment, will appear in the menu along with other styles. Remember that you can also change the name of a predefined style using the **Rename style** option from the option menu in the **Styles** pane. Insert a name for your style, then select the option **Include Layer Blending Options,** and press **OK.**

9. Click on the **Styles** option to verify that the new style you just created appears in the sample list, and after that press **OK** to return to the document and thereby finish this exercise.

052

After entering a name and specifying whether to include the effects and layer blending options, your new style will appear at the bottom of the Styles gallery samples.

Note that each of the default styles has some blending options with some specific characteristics that you can modify to create your own styles.

Creating masks

WITH THE MASK SETTINGS you can easily and quickly create and edit masks. The mask settings, included in this version of Photoshop, are in the new Properties panel. They have the tools needed to create vector-based and pixel-based masks. You can adjust mask density and edit feathering, simply select non-continous objects, and so on.

1. To perform this exercise, we recommend using an image similar to the example. (You can download this one, called **053.jpg**, from our website). With the **Magic Wand Tool**, select the pixels with the same color. (In the example we selected the yellow petals of the flowers.) If it fails at first, play with the functions **Add to Selection** and **Subtract from Selection** to achieve the desired selection.

2. In the **Properties** pane, click the third icon in the second row, which corresponds with the **Black & White** option.

3. As you know, to apply settings from the **Adjustments** panel, add a layer mask to the **Layers** panel. Click the second icon

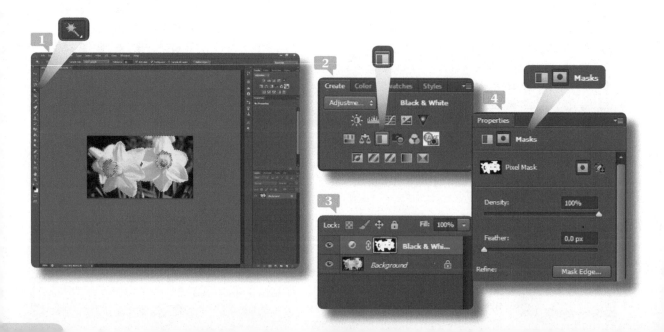

located under the **Properties** tab  to access the features of masks and see the available settings for the pixels mask.

4. You can show and hide the layer mask by clicking on the eye that appears at the bottom of the Properties pane. Try it.

5. Then, click the **Invert** button in the Properties pane to invert the pixels covered by the mask layer, see now, how the **Black & White** layer mask works. Now repress the **Invert** button.

6. Here we show that the effect can be somewhat blurred by increasing the value of the **Feather** field. Drag the slider to the right of this field to a value of about **10**.

7. Finally, you will improve the effect of the mask. Click the **Mask Edge** button.

8. It is accessed from the **Refine Mask** dialog box, where it is possible to improve the quality of the edges of a selection and display it in several modes that facilitate editing. You see that by default the selection is displayed on a white background. We will increase the size to further smooth the edge of the selection with a uniform blur. Double-click the **Feather** field and insert a value of **5**.

9. To finish, you will sharpen the soft edges of the selection. Double-click the **Contrast** field, enter a value of **20** and press the **OK** button to apply the new settings to the edges of the mask.

Creating compositions with masks

MASKS LET YOU ISOLATE AND PROTECT parts of an image, hiding or showing them. To do this, after selecting an area you can use the Vector Mask or Create Clipping Mask.

1. In this exercise, we will create two compositions with images **054_1.jpg, 054_2.jpg, 054_3.jpg, and 054_4.jpg,** which can be download from our website and stored in the images folder on your computer. To begin, open the first two images and convert the background layers to regular layers.

2. In image **054_2.jpg,** click the thumbnail layer while holding down the **Ctrl** key to select everything and press the key combination **Ctrl + C** to copy it.

3. Select **054_1.jpg,** create a new layer by pressing the sixth icon in the **Layers** panel and paste in the contents of the clipboard by pressing the **Ctrl + V.**

4. You now have two layers. You want the ball from Layer 0 showing on Layer 1. But first, use the transform tools you already know to reposition and resize the image in Layer 1.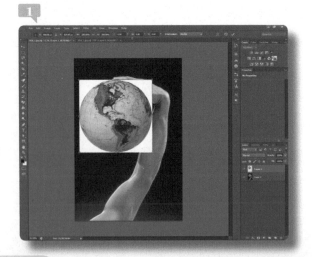

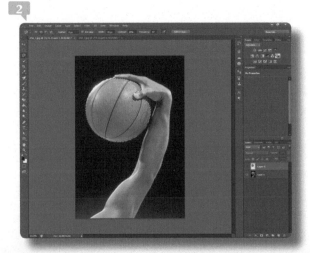

5. Hide Layer 1 by clicking its visibility icon, while in Layer 0 use a selection tool to select the ball. 2

6. Show and activate Layer 1 then click the third icon in the **Layers** pane, which corresponds to the **Add layer mask.**

7. When you have achieved the effect with the mask that you want, see how it displays in the Layers panel. 3 Then use the **Brush Tool** with the foreground color black to paint on the mask half of the ball, then save the resulting image in the Photoshop format. 4

8. Now open **054_3.jpg** and **054_4.jpg** and, after converting their backgrounds to regular layers, paste the contents of the second image in a new layer of the first image by repeating the previous steps.

9. Use the free transform tool to increase the width of the map image and hide that layer.

10. Once on Layer 0, select the arm (you can do this by selecting the background and invert the selection) and copy it by pressing **Ctrl + C**. Then press the **Ctrl + J** to create a new layer from the copy.

11. Now display and select Layer 1, open the **Layer** menu and choose **Create Clipping Mask.** 5

12. See the clipping mask behavior both in the image and in the **Layers** panel. Reduce the fill to **25%** in the **Fill** field. 6

IMPORTANT

A vector mask creates a form with sharp edges while a layer clipping mask allows you to use the contents of a mask layer above it.

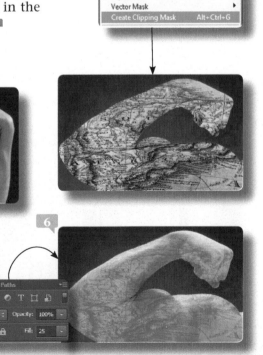

Applying artistic and sketch filters

PHOTOSHOP HAS FIFTEEN artistic filters, each of which has predetermined characteristics that can be changed prior to their application. The Sketch filters are used to add a specific texture to images, often giving the effect of a hand-drawn sketch. Photoshop has fourteen different types of filters for sketching.

1. To perform this exercise you can use any photo you have stored on your computer or you can use the sample file **055.jpg,** which as always is located in the download area of our website. Open the **Filter** menu, click on the **Artistic** command and choose **Poster Edges.**

2. A dialog box appears for **Poster Edges** with options to increase or decrease the border thickness, intensity, or rasterization. On the left you can see a sample of this image with the selected filter already applied. To see the entire preview image, click the arrow button for the field that shows the percentage of display and choose **Fit in view.**

3. Continue by modifying one of the filters. Double-click the field **Edge Intensity,** insert, for example, the value **4,** and press **OK** to see the final result.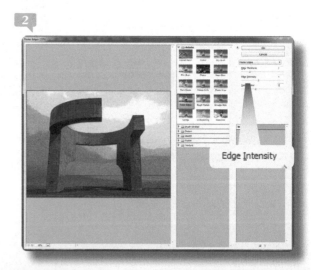

4. On the same image add a new filter to accentuate the artistic detail of the image surface, as if it were covered with shiny plastic. Open the **Filter** menu, click on the **Artistic** command and choose **Plastic Wrap**.

5. Play around with the controls of this filter and click **OK** to apply. 3

6. Now we'll use the **History** pane to override the filter applications, so that the image returns to its original appearance. Open the **Window** menu and click the **History** option.

7. In the **History** pane, click **Open** to recover the image as it was originally opened. 4 Hide this panel by clicking the double arrow on the header.

8. Note that the combination of Sketch filters can actually damage the composition rather than improve it. Open the **Filter** menu, click on the **Sketch** command and choose the **Conté Crayon** filter. 5

9. This filter reproduces the particular type of texture made by the Conté Crayon. Double-click the **Background** field **Level** and insert the value **10**.

10. Play with the **Texture** controls section and click **OK** to apply the filter and see the result in the image. 6

IMPORTANT

The amount of time it takes to apply these filters depends on the processing ability of your computer and the image size. Obviously, depending on the characteristics of each image, you can get different effects depending on the type of filter applied and the parameters established for them.

The **History** pane allows you to retrieve previous image states before the filters were applied.

Getting to know the new Blur filters

BLUR FILTERS ARE SOME OF THE MOST USED FILTERS in Photoshop. While their primary function is to soften a selection or a particular object, they are also very useful for creating spectacular effects used as a background or to get a sense of movement. Photoshop CS6 has a dramatic change with respect to these filters. With these filters, Field Blur, Blur, and Tilt Change, it is now possible to indicate which part of the image you want to blur, to what degree, and the direction of the blur.

1. Download image **056.jpg** from our website and, having stored it in your images folder, open it in Photoshop. What we want you to do here is to blur practically all the image except for the woman's head. To do this, use the new blurring features of Photoshop CS6. Pull down the **Filter** menu and click on the category **Blur** filters.

2. The first three options are those corresponding to the new blur filters. Click on the **Field Blur** and see what happens.

3. On the right side of the window of the program two new panels are loaded: **Blur Tools,** from which you can change

the management of the blur, and **Blur Effects** which lets you manage the light and color involved in the process. As you have selected the **Field Blur,** this is the kind of blur you can see marked in the first pane. The image also is completely out of focus, while the cursor takes on the appearance of a spike. The focus, located by default in the center of the image, allows us to place the center of the blur where you are most interested. Click on the face of the woman to change this location.

4. Then from the **Blur Tools** panel, you can increase or decrease the amount of blur in the indicated area. Move the **Blur** slider to the right to increase the amount of blurring and to the left to decrease it. Insert a value of **0 px** to clear the blur in the area indicated.

5. In the **Blur Tools** pane click the arrow for the **Iris Blur** option.

6. A circle appears in the center of the screen. You can locate and shape according to our blur preferences. Click the center of the circle on the focus, and drag it to the approximate center of the woman's chin, then click the handle at the top of the circle and drag it upward until you get an ellipse. Play around with the **Blur** field control to increase or decrease the amount of blur.

IMPORTANT

When you are working with this type of **Iris Blur** filter, you can change the center of the blur to a square. To do this, drag the small square-shaped handle located on the outer circle.

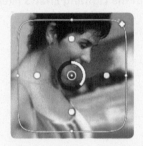

After modifying with the new blur filters, click on the **OK** button on the Options Bar, if you click on the undo button, which is shown with a curved arrow pointing to the left, the image returns to its original appearance. The **Cancel** button abandons the image editing mode.

If the **Preview** option in the Options Bar is enabled, changes will be able to check the changes as they are executed.

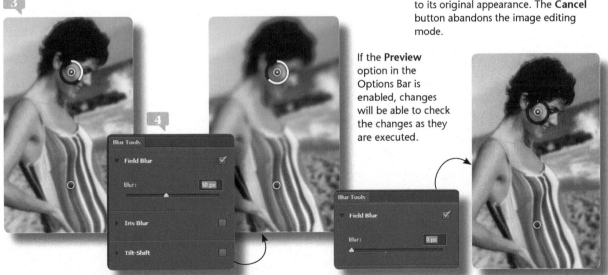

Applying paint and light effects

STYLE FILTERS LET YOU APPLY PAINTING EFFECTS to displace the pixels or enhance the contrast of an image. For their part, filters let you interpret the effect of light on an object and create pockets of light that increase an image's realism.

1. To perform this exercise you can use image **057.jpg** find on our website. Open it in Photoshop, pull down the **Filter** menu, click on the command and choose **Stylize**, and then the **Emboss** option.

2. This filter displays the image with an elevated effect and uses gray fill colors that are combined with the fill color of the original image. ▶ In the filter dialog box, you can change the angle, height, and amount of relief. In the **Height** field, enter the value **5** and click **OK**.

3. To preserve the color and detail when applied to the **Emboss** effect, you can use the **Fade** command after applying the filter. Let's look at how you do that: Pull down the **Edit** menu and select the **Fade Emboss** option. ▶

4. In the **Fade** box, insert a value of **70** in the **Opacity** field and press **OK**. ▶

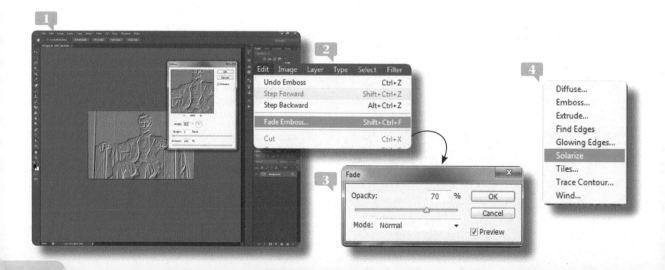

057

5. Then pull down the **Filter** menu, click on the **Stylize** command and select the **Solarize** option.

6. The **Solarize** effect lets you blend a negative with a positive image. You cannot modify any of the settings of this option. You will continue to apply other filters, but first, recover the original appearance of the image from the **History** pane.

7. From the **Filter** menu, click on the **Stylize** command and select the **Tiles** option.

8. In the **Number Of Tiles** field, insert the value as **30,** click the **Foreground Color** button so that the background color of the mosaic is the same as the foreground color currently selected in the Tools pane and click **OK** to apply the filter.

9. To recover the original look of the image, use the **Filter** menu, select the **Render** category and choose **Difference Clouds.**

10. This filter creates a concentrated cloud, using random colors and is based on both the foreground and background colors. You will now add a flash to the image. Open the **Filter** menu, click the **Render** command and choose **Lens Flare.**

11. The chosen filter applies a bright area simulating the refraction of a camera. Enter in the **Shine** field a value of **120,** choose **105 mm Prime Lens Type,** reposition the flash in the preview pane where you want it and press **OK** to apply the filter and see the effect it has on the image.

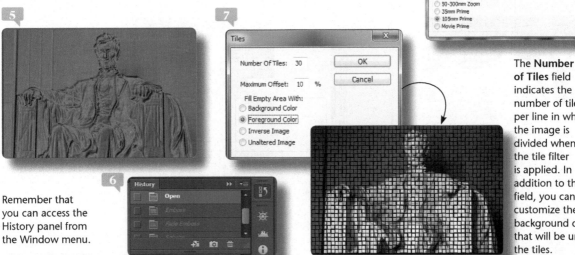

Remember that you can access the History panel from the Window menu.

The **Number of Tiles** field indicates the number of tiles per line in which the image is divided when the tile filter is applied. In addition to this field, you can customize the background color that will be under the tiles.

Getting to know the light and shadow effects

OCCASIONALLY IT MAY BE APPROPRIATE THAT, as well as applying filters, we also want to change light and shade settings, and the color settings of the objects included in the composition that are affected by the effect of light applied. One of the special effects lighting that best sets the tone and brightness of objects in a composition is the Lens Flare filter, which we applied in the previous exercise. The options for this filter are very broad: it is possible to apply a flash as a brilliance point, or with a large radius of action, as a focus or point of light that will force a change in the color of the image.

1. In this lesson you will apply special effects on the light and shade complemented by adjustments of the hue, saturation and brightness on the sample image **058.jpg** that, as always, can be copied from our website and stored in your images folder. Apply the Difference Clouds filter on the image. **1** Open the **Filter** menu, click the **Render** command and select **Lens Flare.** **2**

2. This time, in the **Lens Flare** dialog box, select the type of lens as **35 mm Prime.** **3**

3. Also, increase the brightness of the flare. Double-click the **Brightness** field, enter the value **150** and, after repositioning the flash in the picture, press **OK**.

4. Notice the new look of the image.  Since the light is different, you will also modify the brightness of the object. Pull down the **Image** menu, click the **Adjustments** command and select **Curves.**

5. In the **Curves** dialog box modify the tonal range of the image. Drag the tone curve to achieve the desired effect and click **OK** to apply the changes.

6. To finish this exercise, and to check other possible effects of light, create a new brightness effect. Select the **Filter** menu again, click the **Render** command and select the **Lighting Effects.**

7. New to this version of Photoshop CS6, the filter loads, instead of the **Lighting Effects** dialog box, the corresponding pane, and the **3D** pane. From the start, you can choose the type of light (focus, point, or infinite) as well as parameters such as intensity, color, brightness, etc. Choose **Infinife** in the **Type** field, then manipulate the smaller handle that appears in the center of the image to change the lighting.

8. Play around with the different parameters in the properties panel to get the lighting that best suits your preferences. When finished, press the **OK** button in the Options Bar.

IMPORTANT

From the Lighting Effects properties pane, you can choose the color of light you want to color the image with. We recommend that you experiment with different tones by clicking on the **Color** sample field and selecting different colors from the Color Picker box.

Pixelating and applying textures

THE FILTERS INCLUDED IN THE CATEGORIES Pixelate and Texture make the image truly pictorial. The Pixelate filters allow you to split or compact the pixels in cells with similar values. As such, these filters let you apply a concrete texture such as canvas, cloth, crumpled paper or, depth to an image.

1. To perform this exercise, use an image with a uniform background like the one you used in the previous exercise. You can retrieve it from the **History** panel. Open the **Filter** menu, click on the **Pixelate** category and choose **Crystallize.**

2. This filter allows you to group the pixels in a solid color in the shape of a polygon. By default, these polygons are displayed with a cell size of 10. Enter a value of **6** in the **Cell Size** field, then click **OK.**

3. Next, select the background and apply a texture. With the **Magic Wand Tool** and establishing a tolerance of 60 pixels, choose the background image.

059

4. Pull down the **Filter** menu, click on the **Texture** category and select **Craquelure.**

5. This filter creates a plaster surface. Double-click the **Crack Spacing** field, enter the value **54** to increase the space ostensibly,  and then press **OK.**

6. Pull down the **Filter** menu, select **Brush Strokes**, and then select the **Sprayed Strokes** option.

7. This filter paints a picture using the dominant colors with traces of colored angled spray. Change the radius and the direction of the line and press **OK** to apply the effect.

8. You will add the ultimate effect of this exercise to the background. Again, pull down the **Filter** menu, click on the **Brush Strokes** category and select **Angled Strokes.**

9. This filter re-colors the image using the dominant colors while accentuating the angular strokes. You can select the path direction and intensity. This time, you will reduce the balance of direction so that the lines are not very visible. Double-click the **Direction Balance** field, enter a value of **20** and then press **OK.**

10. Press the **Ctrl + D** to deselect the background and **Ctrl + S** to save the changes.

IMPORTANT

In the case of 3D textures, Photoshop lets you edit them with the adjustment tools and paint. The textures of 3D files as 2D files are imported with the file and appear as entries in the 3D layer.

The settings box for the **Sprayed Strokes** filter lets you change the length, radius, and direction of the stroke.

Warping images

PHOTOSHOP ALLOWS YOU TO DISTORT IMAGES quickly and easily. The Warp option, included in the Transform command from the Edit menu, allows you to easily create an image that will wrap around any figure. This technique allows you to contort the image size by stretching, bending, or undulating the shape.

1. The objective of this exercise is to create a label that fits another object, namely, a cone, so we recommend using images **060_1.jpg** and **060_2.jpg**. You can download these from our website and keep a copy in your images folder. Place the second image in the foreground, select the background image and invert the selection, so that only the arrow is selected. 🔲

2. Copy the selection by pressing **Ctrl + C,** put the first file in the foreground. Then press **Ctrl + V** to paste the copied image selection. 🔲

3. The poster is pasted onto a new layer. With this layer selected, and before distorting it, reduce the size to 40% of the original size by inserting this value in the **H** and **W** fields in the Options Bar. Then select the **Scale** command.

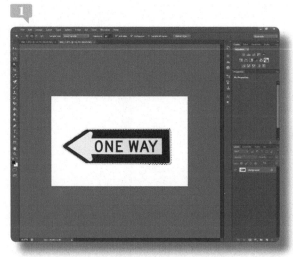

If you forget any part of how to select an object, please review exercises 18–23.

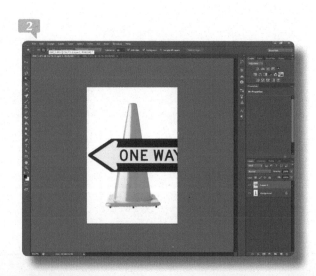

060

4. Next, open the **Edit** menu, click on the **Transform** command and choose **Warp**.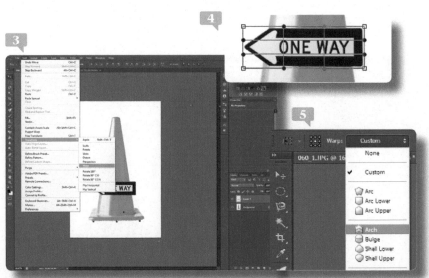

5. The image has been defined by a series of handles and a grid that allow you to manipulate the image. In the **Options Bar,** open the **Warp** field and choose **Arch.**

6. The slope of the curve, top and bottom, should be in the opposite direction, which is the default. Double-click the field **Bend**, type a value of approximately –20% and press **Return.**

7. You can play with the value of the curve until it is perfectly matched to the object. You will now modify the dimensions of the label. In the **Options Bar,** click the third icon from the right to switch between free transform mode and transformation mode.

8. The dimensions of the selected image can be modified using the values in the appropriate fields or by dragging the handles. In this case, keep the Shift key pressed to manipulate the size proportionally. The image will decrease until the label fits snugly over the cone.

9. Click the **Commit transform** icon to accept the changes and see the finished result.

You can deform an object by dragging the handles or by applying a predetermined form offered by Photoshop.

Using vanishing points for editing images

THE VANISHING POINT OPTION in the Filter menu offers a new way to modify or distort images from their perspective. With the Vanishing Point filter, you specify the image planes that you will apply the editing to, and which ones will respect the persepective of the plane they work in.

1. To perform this exercise, use an image of a tower or other tall building in perspective as in the sample file, **061.jpg.** You will extend the height of the building further while maintaining the perspective. Keep in mind that you can keep the results of this filter in the same layer of the image or on a separate layer, which should be created before selecting the filter. The latter option is useful when you want to preserve the original image and use the opacity controls, styles, and layer blending modes. Create a new layer from the **Layers** panel. **1**

2. After you have created a new layer, where you will place the results of the filter, open the **Filter** menu and choose the **Vanishing Point** option. **2**

3. The Filter dialog box appears, which allows you to complete the process. **3** In the Tools palette, you will find that **Create Plane** is activated, and you will add the different planes to

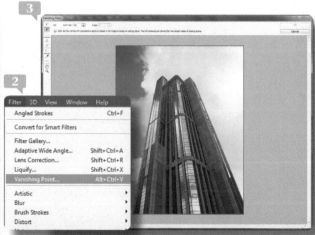

delimit the part of the image you want to clone, that is, the reference area for the expansion of the building. To do this, define the four corner nodes by clicking on the preview. **4**

4. By inserting the last point, the program detects that you want make a square around a given area and displays a blue grid. If red, you should adjust it by the handles, as it means that the perspective is not well defined and, therefore, would not give an optimal result. Once this area is defined, repeat the action, though this time with the Selection Tool. This will help the program to memorize the content to be cloned. In the Tools palette, click the **Marquee Tool**, whose icon displays a rectangle. **5**

5. Double-click on the perspective plane to create the selection area.

6. Following instructions from the top of the box, press the **Alt** key and drag the selection to copy it to another destination. **6**

7. As you can see, it has added the selected area to the point that you indicated, obtaining an extension to the building height. You can correct small defects with the **Stamp Tool** dialog box, and continue editing the image in Photoshop. Click the **OK** button to apply the filter permanently.

Correcting lens distortion

IN MANY CASES, PHOTOGRAPHS show defects of lens distortion, which produce spheroids (straight lines that are curved at the edges of the image) and pincushion distortion (straight lines that curve inward). You can correct these defects in Photoshop CS6 using the Lens Correction filter and the new adjustable wide angle filter, which are included in this latest version of the program.

1. To perform this exercise, you can use image **062.jpg,** which can be found in the download area of our website. Once you have copied this file to your images folder, open it in Photoshop and make sure the image has a slight pincushion distortion and that it is also somewhat tilted. You will correct these defects with the **Lens Correction** filter. Activate it from the **Filter** menu.

2. This opens the properties box of the filter that can be used to correct the lens defects described above, and also to rotate an image or correct your perspective more accurately than with the transformation tools. First, you will correct the lens distortion. You can do this manually using the first icon in the tool palette in this window or setting new values in the **Custom** tab.Select that tab and drag it slightly to the left of the **Remove Distortion** slider until it reaches the value –4.

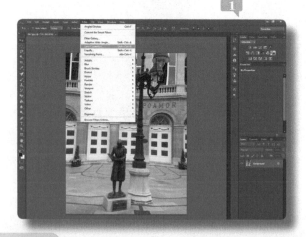

062

3. Watch how it improves the image. To use the **Remove Distortion Tool** from the **Lens Correction** box you must drag it slightly toward the center of the image or to its edges and see how it reduces distortion. After correcting this first fault of the lens, you will now straighten the image. Select the **Straighten Tool,** the second icon in the Tools panel. 🔳

4. If you want to work more accurately, turn on the **Show Grid** option. 🔳

5. Then by dragging, draw a straight line along the upper door frames and see how, by releasing the mouse button, the perspective of the image is automatically corrected. 🔳

6. You can enable and disable the **Preview** filter box to see the state of the changes and compare the original image with the retouched one. You can also adjust the zoom display of the image to have a better idea of what the necessary corrections are. On the other hand, if you think you have other images taken with the same camera and with the same defects, you can save your settings 🔳 to automatically reapply them to these images. Press the **OK** button to apply the filter.

IMPORTANT

Keep in mind that the **Lens Correction** filter only works with images of 8 and 16 bits per channel in RGB or Grayscale.

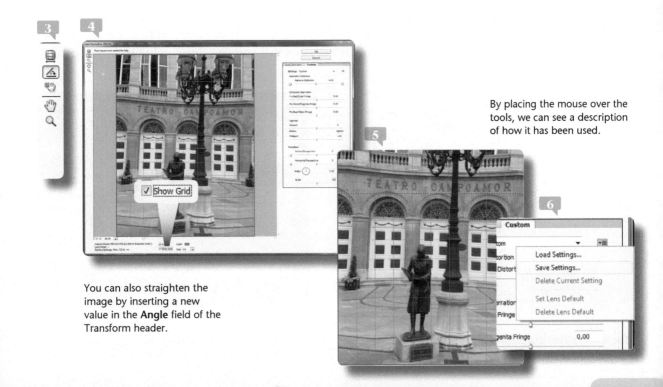

By placing the mouse over the tools, we can see a description of how it has been used.

You can also straighten the image by inserting a new value in the **Angle** field of the Transform header.

Correcting red-eye

HOW OFTEN IN FLASH PHOTOGRAPHY does a person appear with red eyes? This disturbing effect is easily fixed by the simple Red Eye Tool, found in the Tools panel, which shares space with the correction brushes and Patch Tool. Once activated, simply draw a rectangle around the pupil or click directly on it and immediately, the program performs the correction. In the Options Bar, you can adjust the size of the pupil and the amount of darkness, if the initial result is not satisfactory.

1. In this exercise, we will show you the simple procedure to correct red-eye in a photograph. For this, use an image with this problem (if desired you can use the sample file, **063.jpg**) and extend your zoom to work more comfortably. Click on the arrow located on the seventh Tool in the tool pane and select the **Red Eye Tool.** 🔲

2. The **Options Bar** shows only two fields: **Pupil Size** and **Darken Amount,** 🔲 set both to 50%. To correct the effect of the left eye, click on the pupil. 🔲

3. As you can see, the result is immediate. If the color of the pupil changes but does not appear completely black, you can in-

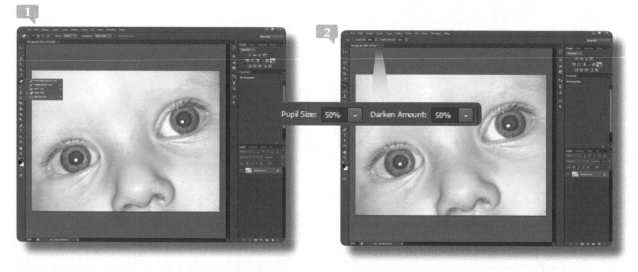

The **Red Eye Tool** shares space in the Tools panel with the Healing Brush and Patch Tools.

The default values selected by the **Red Eye Tool** are usually adequate to obtain the best results.

crease the **Darken Amount** field. The **Pupil Size** field, in turn, increases or reduces the area affected by the tool. Double-click the **Darken Amount** field, type the value **80** and press **Return** to confirm the change.

4. Click on the pupil of the right eye and see how it is automatically applied.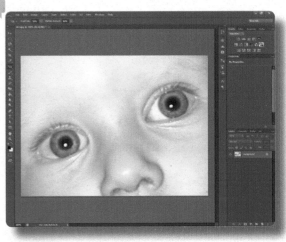

5. Remember that the **Red Eye Tool** also allows you to eliminate white and green reflections that often appear in photographs of animals that were taken with flash. To end this very simple practice, close the image and save the changes in it. Press the **blade** of the tab image and in the dialog box that appears, click the **Yes** button to store the changes.

6. Keep the default options set to JPEG and press the **OK** button to finish the exercise.

The red-eye effect occurs due to a reflection of the camera flash in the retina of the subject. It is often more evident in photographs taken in dark rooms because the iris is fully open. To reduce the effect, use the red-eye reduction on your camera, use a separate flash drive, or perform the necessary retouching with Photoshop.

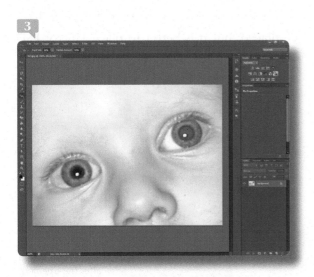

Modify the amount of darkness and pupil size for even more professional results. The quantity of darkening sets the tone correction, and pupil size increases or decreases the area that will be affected by the tool.

Adobe Photoshop CS6 Extended

Save changes to the Adobe Photoshop document "063.jpg" before closing?

Yes   No   Cancel

Working with Smart Objects

SMART OBJECTS ARE THE SOLUTION to preserve the image data and record changes that are previewed only when combined with the image layers. They are layers containing image data derived from vector or raster images that keep their original features without danger of losing information when editing them. They can be created from the Open as Smart Object command from the File menu, which makes a smart object layer by placing a file or pasting data from Illustrator. An icon is placed in the bottom right corner of the layer thumbnail to indicate that this is a Smart Object.

1. To begin, click the **File** menu and click on the **Open as Smart Object.**

2. In the **Open as a Smart Object** box, locate and select the image you want to work with and click **Open.**

3. Note that in the **Layers** panel, it appears a thumbnail of the image, in the left corner of the layer. Now use the **Place** option to import a file as a Smart Object in this Photoshop image. Open the **File** menu and click on the **Place** option.

4. JPEG files can be placed, but it is better to place TIFF or PSD

The layers created after the opening of an image as a Smart Object use the name of the source file in question.

files because these file types allow you to add layers, change pixels, and save the file without any data loss. In the **Place** box, locate and select one of your .psd images and click **Place**.

5. Reposition and resize the image if necessary and finally, to insert the image as a Smart Object, double-click on it.

6. The Smart Object icon also appears in the thumbnail of the new layer. Now you will create a regular layer that will be converted to a Smart Object. Create a new layer, click the **Layer** menu, click on the **Smart Objects** option and select **Convert to Smart Object**.

7. You can find this same option in the contex menu of the layer or in the **Layers** panel options. Smart Objects allow you to change the scale of a layer, rotate and deform without losing the quality of the original image data. However, it is not possible to perform operations that affect the pixel data, such as overexposure, underexposure, or cloning, among others. Select the **Brush Tool** in the Tools pane and click on the image.

8. The box that appears warns us that in order to edit the layer with this tool, it is necessary to rasterize the image and thereby turn the layer into a regular layer. Press the **OK** button to rasterize the image and finish the exercise.

Using Smart Filters

IMPORTANT

To **expand** or **collapse** the view of intelligent filters applied, use the arrowhead to the right of the selected layer. Also, if you want to change the blending options or characteristics of the filter simply double-click on the icon to the right of the filter or on the name.

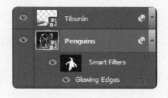

FILTERS THAT ARE APPLIED to a Smart Object and Smart Filters are listed in the Layers panel under the layer to which they have been applied. They aren't destructive because they can be adjusted, eliminated, or hidden without affecting the original object. The image settings for Shadows/Lighting, HDR Tones, and Variations can also be applied as Smart Filters. Smart Filters are applied to a Smart Object layer or only a selected part of the image. It is also possible to apply a Smart Filter to a regular layer using the Convert for Smart Filters in the Filter menu.

1. To begin, apply an artistic filter to a layer with a Smart Object. You can use the file **065.psd**, which can be found on our website. Select the **Shark** layer, open the **Filter** menu, click on the **Artistic** option and select **Plastic Wrap**. **1**

2. A box appears with the filtering options. Click in the field to the right of the slider **Smoothness** to increase this effect, then click the **OK** button to apply a Smart Filter. **2**

3. Notice how the filter is applied and at the same time it appears under the selected layer in the **Layers** pane. **3** The eye-shaped

icon appears to the left of the filters, which allows us to show or hide them. You then apply the filter to a specific area of the **Penguins** smart layer. Activate it and with the **Quick Selection Tool**, select one of the penguins.

4. Open the **Filter** menu, click on the option **Stylize** and choose the **Glowing Edges** filter.

5. In the box filter options, click on the right of the slider of the field that increases **Edge Width**. By pressing on the right edge of the slider, it will also increase the brightness. To apply the effect, press the **OK** button.

6. Observe the **Layers** panel. The Smart Filter has been applied as a mask in the selected area only. In the event that there are several Smart Filters, you can easily rearrange them by dragging on the panel. Similarly, you can delete them by dragging them to the trash at the bottom of the panel or by using the appropriate option from the Context menu. You can also use this menu option to disable them temporarily or change its parameters. To finish this exercise, press the blade of the image tab and in the dialog box that appears, click the **Yes** button to sve the changes.

The eye icon next to Smart Filters can shown or hidde them.

Drawing with the Pen tools

WITH THE PEN TOOL you can draw lines and curves called paths. Paths can form objects with a color fill or be supplemented with a style layer. The Freeform Pen Tool, meanwhile, lets you draw freehand, without any limitation to form.

1. For this exercise you can use image **066.jpg** that, as always, can be found in the download area of our website. Select the **Pen Tool**, represented by the drawing of a fountain pen, from the Tools pane. 🗨1

2. In Photoshop CS6 there has been a slight modification to the appearance of the **Pen Tool** options. Pull down the options for the **Path** field and select the option for **Shape** mode. 🗨2

3. The **Fill** field of the **Options Bar** indicates the fill color of the figure and in the **Style** field, the style that will be applied to the figure. Choose white as the fill color 🗨3 and click on the image to create different anchor points until you obtain an irregular shape that you will retouch so that it imitates a cloud. 🗨4

4. After creating the layout, try applying, for example, the **Paint Bucket Tool**. Turn it on in the Tools pane, click inside the irregular shape, and in the warning box that appears, click the **OK** button to rasterize the layer.

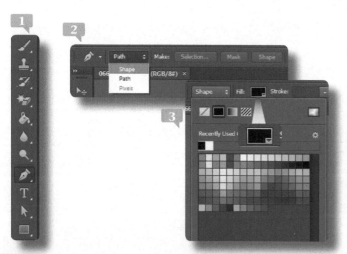

5. The layer becomes rasterized automatically, and so, you can now modify the fill color. Click the Options button in the **Layers** panel and choose **Blending Options.**

6. In the **Layer Style** panel, click the option to select **Gradient Overlay** and keep the gradient formed from black and white. Press the **OK** button.

7. You will also apply a blur filter to make it lightly blurred. Open the **Filter** menu, click the **Blur** option and then choose **Blur Motion.**

8. In the **Motion Blur** box increase the value of the **Distance** field and press **OK.**

9. In the second part of this exercise you will see how to use the **Freeform Pen Tool**. In the Tools pane, click the arrow button on the **Pen Tool**, select the above tool and draw an irregular shape by dragging.

10. Objects created with this tool don't have visable anchor points by default, and they are filled with the current background color. To change the shape of the object, you can make the anchor points visible and change their position with the **Add Anchor Point Tool**, which is included in the same group of Pen Tools. To finish, reduce the amount of fill of the new object by inserting a value less than 100 in the **Fill** field in the **Layers** panel. After you have done this, save the document.

IMPORTANT

The advantage of the **Freeform PenTool** is that as you draw, the program will automatically include anchor points, so that once you have completed the drawing it may be amended. You can add and delete anchor points on a form created with the Freeform Pen Tool by using the Add Anchor Point Tool.

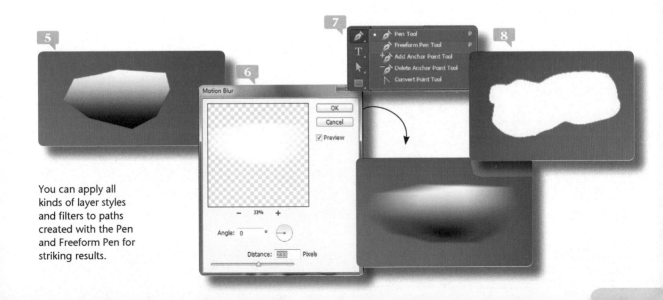

You can apply all kinds of layer styles and filters to paths created with the Pen and Freeform Pen for striking results.

Adding text to a path

IMPORTANT

As you move or change the shape of the path that acts as a path, the text will wrap to the new location or new form.

THE TEXT PATH IS OBTAINED after performing two basic steps: the creation of a shape by using a drawing tool, such as the Pen Tool, and the introduction of the text. You can use the Freeform Pen Tool, since it lets you draw a line, for example, a picture element.

1. Your goal this time is to create a freehand path that loops through a figure, then to add a short amount of text onto that path. You can use the same image that you used in the previous exercise or any other image. To begin, select the **Freeform Pen Tool**.

2. To create a freehand path you must use the drag technique, but before that, you will activate an option that will allow the line to fit the image. In the **Options Bar,** click the **Magnetic.** option.

3. Click on the arrowhead accompanying the icon to the left of the **Magnetic** option.

4. In this panel you can set preferences for the path from the image. The **Width** field lets you assign the margin, in pixels, within which the pen can draw, the **Contrast** field specifies the percentage of possible contour image, and the **Screen**

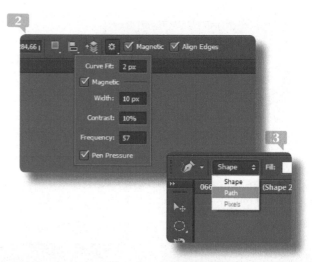

067

Ruling field controls the number of anchor points to be inserted in the path, between 5 (more points) and 40 (less points). Double-click in the **Width** field, enter the value **3** then press **Return.**

5. To draw a line, display the field showing **Shape** and choose, in this case, the **Path** option.

6. By previously activating the **Magnetic** option, the pointer, as well as taking the form of a fountain pen, will also show a small magnet. Click a starting point in your image, drag the shape to create the path and press **Return** when done.

7. You already have the path or trajectory, now let's insert the text. Select the **Horizontal Type Tool** in the Tools pane and click on the point considered the center of the track.

8. Check that, as in any other case of insertion of text, the program has created a new layer. Directly write the sample phrase (not forgetting to adjust the font size to the dimensions of the image) and press the key combination **Ctrl + Return** to confirm.

You have now created a text path. From here, you can edit the text in all aspects: size, font, alignment, style, and so on. Remember that in any case you previously selected the **Horizontal Type Tool.**

Drawing geometric shapes

IMPORTANT

You can type text into a geometric shape using the Text Tool. Once inserted, you can modify its properties (size, color, alignment, etc.) as usual.

PHOTOSHOP ALLOWS YOU TO DRAW basic geometric shapes such as rectangles, rounded rectangles, ellipses, polygons, and lines, as well as customized shapes. Using any of the basic preset forms, creates a shape layer. New in this version of Photoshop CS6, basic geometric shapes are no longer part of the Pen Tool, but are accessible only from the Tools panel.

1. In this exercise you will use some of the commands available for geometric shapes. To begin, click the arrowhead of the **Rectangle Tool**, the eighteenth icon in the tool palette, then select the **Line Tool**. 🗨1

2. From the **Options Bar** you can set the characteristics of the shape you want to draw. Double-click the **Weight** field. In order to increase the thickness of the line, enter the value **5** and press **Return**. 🗨2

3. The color is assigned to any form that is active on the board of tools such as background color. In this case, pull down the color display panel and select the **Fill** field and choose **black** as our fill color. 🗨3

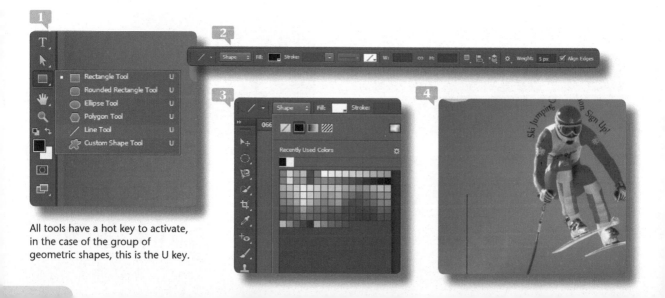

All tools have a hot key to activate, in the case of the group of geometric shapes, this is the U key.

4. The command displays a white and a red line diagonally that allows you to apply a different color for the outline of the shape. To draw the line on our image, click and drag until you have the desired length. 4

5. Once you have inserted the form, you can modify both the width and length from the **W** and **H** fields respectively, which you will find in the Options Bar. Then draw a new figure, which will be inserted into a new shape layer. In the Tool palette, display the **Line Tool** and choose the **Polygon Tool**. 5

6. The **Polygon Tool** is used to adjust the number of sides the shape will have, which will in turn depend on the purpose of the composition. In this case, to draw a triangle, double-click the field **Sides** in the **Options Bar,** enter the value 3 and then press **Return.** 6

7. Now, mark the triangle by dragging and placing it above the line, as a sign. (To reposition the form accurately, use the **Move Tool.**) 7

8. A new layer appears in the **Layers** panel. 8 Select the fill color as white. Display the **Set shape stroke type** and choose a red color to add a trace of this color to our figure. 9

9. Notice the effect achieved 10 and finish the exercise by pressing the key combination **Ctrl + S** to save the changes.

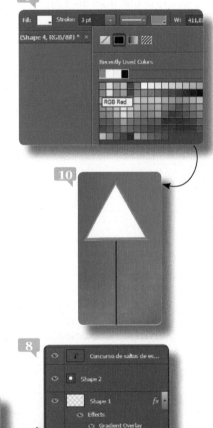

From the **Stroke** field you can increase and decrease the stroke weight of the figure and the next field you can change the type of line shown.

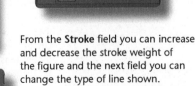

Drawing other forms

IMPORTANT

You can save a customized shape in the library of shapes using the **Define Custom Shape** option from the Edit menu. After naming and saving, the new form will appear in the Forms box.

THE CUSTOM SHAPE TOOL includes a large number of predefined objects and shapes arranged in thematic groups and different aspects: ornaments, animals, tiles, speech bubbles, boxes, arrows, etc. These forms are created as geometric shapes, the color should be selected and the size will be determined when they are drawn on canvas. A custom shape may be stored in order to retrieve it at any time.

1. To work exclusively with custom shapes, add a new layer to the document. ⬛

2. Let's see how to determine the size and color of customized shapes before you create them. In the Tools palette, display the **Polygon Tool** and then click on the **Custom Shape Tool**. ⬛

3. Note that the Options Bar is updated with the settings of the chosen tool. Display the command to the left of **Shape,** then click **Fixed Size.** ⬛

4. You can determine the size in pixels, centimeters, or inches. Type a value of **85 px** in the **W** field, which determines the width, and the same in the **H** field, which determines the height, and then press **Return.** ⬛

Create customized forms new layers of the document so that you can manipulate them independently.

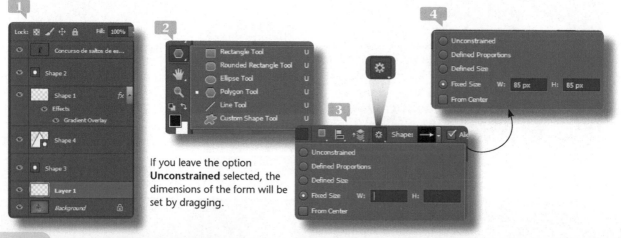

If you leave the option **Unconstrained** selected, the dimensions of the form will be set by dragging.

069

5. Once you have established the size of the custom shape, you will continue the exercise by changing the color. Display the **Fill** field in the Options Bar and choose the color you want. 5

6. Click the arrow button in the **Shape** field in the **Options Bar,** and select the shape you want by double-clicking on it, 6 and then drag it carefully to the place you wish to insert it. 7

7. Let's see where Photoshop keeps its custom shapes. Click the arrow of the **Shape** field and click the round button that has an arrow located at the top right of the box.

8. The list of available forms groups is displayed at the bottom of the menu. Choose, for example, the **Talk Bubbles** group. 8

9. As stated in the warning box that appears, the selected shapes can replace those currently shown in the list or added to it. Press the **OK** button for the group chosen to replace the current forms. 9

10. Those shaps now appear in the chosen category automatically. 10 Remember that if you insert images, they acquire the characteristics of the last set. Complete this exercise by saving the changes in your image.

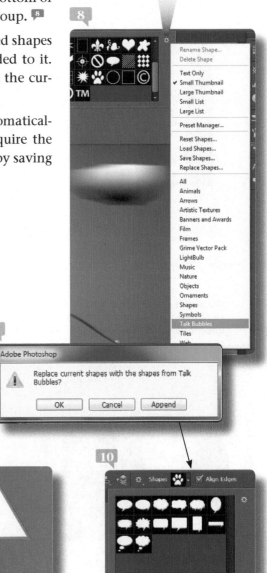

If your document has multiple layers, when you insert a new custom shape and it does not show the fill assigned to it, try rearranging the layers.

Using the Spot Healing Brush

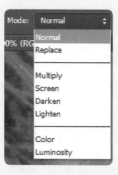
THE SPOT HEALING BRUSH lets you retouch photos with a single click. It is very simple to use: keep the default options and choose a suitable size, just click on the desired effect.

1. In this simple exercise you will see how to fix a flaw in an image with the **Spot Healing Brush Tool.** This tool works similarly to the brush and the clone tools, but it does not require you to select a sample point. The Spot Healing Brush Tool acts by painting pixels from samples in the area around the touch point and matches the texture, lighting, transparency, and shadow of the sampled pixels that must be corrected. To practice using this utility, open an image containing some imperfection or impurity (you can use sample image **070.jpg,** which is found in the download area of our website). Start increasing the zoom of the area. Select the **Zoom Tool** in the **Tools** panel.

2. Click several times in the area of the photograph that you want to retouch to zoom in. In this case, on one of the two eyes.

It is always advisable to zoom in to enlarge the zone containing the imperfection and to be retouched to work more comfortably.

3. The **Spot Healing Brush Tool** shares space in the Tools pane with the **Red Eye Tool, Patch, Healing Brush,** and the new **Content-Aware Patch**. Select it. **3**

4. Keep in mind that a brush that is slightly larger than the area to be corrected will be more effective as it will allow you to cover a larger space with a single keystroke. In any case, you can always use the drag technique to smooth imperfections in a large area. You can choose between three brush options: **Proximity Match, Create Texture**, and **Content-Aware**. **1** The first uses the pixels around the edge of the selection to find an area of the image and use it as a patch on the selected area. The second uses all pixels in the selection to create a tex-ture to correct the area, and the third compares image content closely to perfectly fill the selection and keep the realism of the key details (shadows, borders, and so on). This time, keep the option **Content-Aware** then modify the brush size only. Press the arrow button on the **Brush** field, type in the **Size** field an appropriate value to correct the wart and then press **Return**. **5**

5. Click on the item you want to correct and see the fantastic result. **6**

6. Fix the other imperfections in the image in the same way.

7. Finally, pull down the **View** menu and click on the **Fit on Screen** option.

IMPORTANT

Take note that if your image has several layers, you must activate the **Sample All Layers** option for the program to sample the data from all visible layers. If you deselect this option, data will be sampled from the active layer only.

☑ Sample All Layers

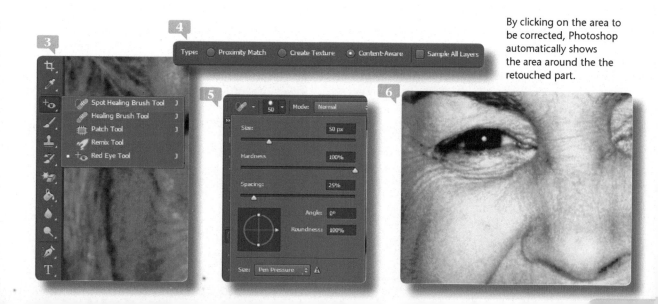

By clicking on the area to be corrected, Photoshop automatically shows the area around the the retouched part.

Mixer Brush. To simulate realistic paintings

PHOTOSHOP HAS SOME TOOLS that generate impressive realistic paint effects. The Mixer Brush is one. With this new brush, it is possible to simulate real painting techniques such as mixing colors on a canvas, combining brushes, or changing the wetness of the painting along a path.

1. To perform this exercise you can use file **071.jpg** which can be copied to your images folder. Once you open the file in Photoshop, create a new layer.

2. Click on the **Arrow Brush Tool** and select the **Mixer Brush Tool.**

3. The **Options Bar** is now set to the selected tool. As you can see, you can customize a large number of brush properties, for example, color, combination merger, wetness, load, mix, etc. Press the arrow button next to the brush size to open the brush picker.

4. In addition to traditional brushes, Photoshop offers configurable bristle tips that look very realistic. Choose the fifth brush in the second row with a double-click.

071

5. The default color of the brush coincides with the selected fore-ground color. Let's change it by taking a sample of the image. Change to the background layer and then while holding down the **Alt** key, click on a petal so that the color is loaded into the brush. 🔲³

6. Go back to Layer 1, click the arrow button for the useful mixer brush combinations, where you see the default **Custom**, and choose **Wet, Heavy Mix**. 🔲⁴

7. Notice how you adjust the values for wet, load, and mix in the **Options Bar** depending on the selected type of mix you are looking for. Now click and drag on one of the flowers to obtain a similar effect in the image. 🔲⁵

8. Take from the background a color swatch of green leaves, and again in Layer 1, brush with the paint mixer in the leaves of the flowers. 🔲⁶

9. Make sure to paint over areas of other colors, since the color blends with the canvas as would happen in a real painting. If the resulting image is to your liking, save it in the Photoshop format.

IMPORTANT

The graphical representation of the chosen type of brush can be turned off using the Show command from the View menu, as long as the graphics card in your computer allows it. You can change the sample position, reduce it, or close it. On the other hand, when you use the brush on your image, you can see the movement reflected in this sample.

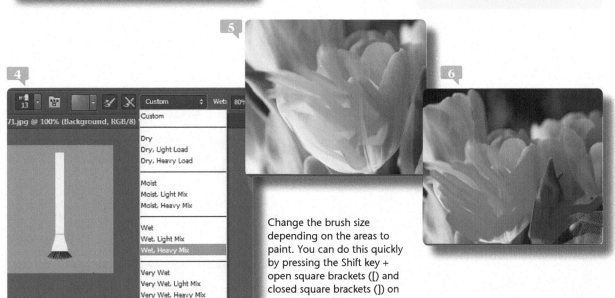

Change the brush size depending on the areas to paint. You can do this quickly by pressing the Shift key + open square brackets ([) and closed square brackets (]) on your keyboard.

Creating and applying custom brushes

YOU CAN MODIFY THE CHARACTERISTICS of the preset brushes as well as create your own types of brushes. Photoshop has the Brush panel, which lets you manipulate the shape, content, and dimensions of any preset brushes. Once modified, the program offers the possibility to save the new brush settings to re-use it when needed.

1. In this lesson you'll learn to manipulate the characteristics of a preset brush so that you can use it in a sample image later on. To begin, create a new layer in the **Layers** panel.

2. Then select the **Brush Tool** in the Tools pane.

3. Press the arrow tip of the brush in the **Options Bar,** open the menu by pressing the round arrow button selector and select the **Special Effect Brushes** category.

4. Click **OK** in the warning box that launches the program to accept the replacement brushes.

5. Go to the **Brush** panel, from which you will carry out the modifications. Pull down the **Window** menu and click on the command **Brush.**

You can also access the Brush panel by pressing the F5 function key.

072

6. Scroll through the samples in the Brush panel with the help of the vertical scroll bar and click on the **brush** type representing a leaf from a tree and showing a size of 84 pixels. **3**

7. The selected brush will help you to create a fallen leaves effect. In the **Size** field, enter a value of **33** and then press **Return**. **4**

8. In the **Angle** field, enter a value of **137** and press **Return**.

9. To increase the spacing between the leaves so that they appear much more scattered, double-click the **Spacing** field, enter **120** and press **Return**. **5**

10. Select the **Shape Dynamics** option to view your options.

11. You will increase the size variation, so that by applying the selected brush leaves appear in different dimensions. Double-click the field **Size Jitter,** type the value **70** and press **Return**.

12. Click on the **Color Dynamics** option, then select the field **Hue Jitter**, then enter a value of **44** and press **Return**. **6**

13. Hide the **Brush** pane by clicking the double arrow in the header.

14. Click the foreground color box in the **Tools** panel, choose a reddish hue in the **Color Picker** box and press **OK**.

15. Click an image point to insert the first item, and while holding down the **Shift** key, click on another point and watch what happens.

IMPORTANT

New to Photoshop CS6, the **Brush** panel presents a new category related to the shape of the brush called Brush Pose. There, you can specify the exact angle, both horizontally and vertically, the rotation, and the pressure of the brush tip.

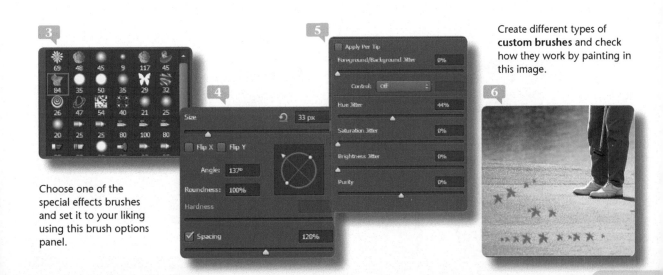

3

4

5

6

Choose one of the special effects brushes and set it to your liking using this brush options panel.

Create different types of **custom brushes** and check how they work by painting in this image.

Optimizing images for the web

ONE OF THE FORMATS USED TO DISPLAY PHOTOGRAPHS on websites or other media is JPEG. Photoshop allows us to optimize images of different formats and convert them to the JPEG format. It also facilitates a quality stabilizer for generated files so you can get up to three JPEG files of varying quality.

1. In this lesson you will learn how to optimize a GIF file, how to convert it to a JPEG file, the standard compression format for images with a continuous tone. For this use an image in that format (if you want, use the file **073.gif**). To begin, open the **File** menu and click **Save for Web & Devices**. 🗩

2. In the **Save for Web & Devices** box, optimized images can be displayed in different formats and with different attributes. From there you can change the optimizing settings while previewing the image so as to apply the settings that best suit our needs. This time, optimize the GIF image to an image with high resolution JPEG format. Click on the arrow button field **Optimized File Format** and then select the **JPEG** format. 🗩

3. Then click the arrow button on the **Compression Quality** field and select **Maximum** quality.

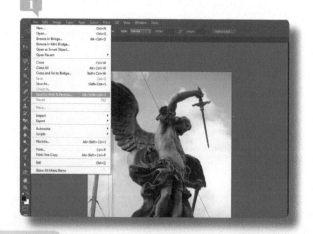

073

4. The **Quality** field now displays a value of 100. You can reduce this value manually to improve compression. The higher quality, the more fully retained the compression algorithm. However, quality results in a larger file, so you must find the right balance between quality and file size. To see the original image and optimized image in the same window, click the tab **2-Up**.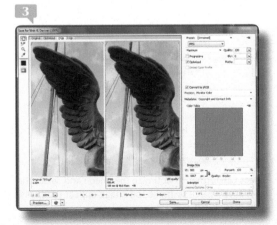

5. You will find the basic data under each image. Since image optimization is usually carried out in order to publish them on websites or on other multimedia, one of these pieces of data is the estimated download time. If desired, Photoshop can automatically create up to three JPEG files of different qualities. Click on the tab **4-Up**.

6. You now have four files starting with the original and ending with the lowest quality. Note the differences in size, download speed, and quality between them. Redisplay only the optimized image by clicking on the **Optimized** tab.

7. Click the button to the right of the download speed and choose **Size/Download Time (2Mbps)**.

8. The download speed decreases dramatically. Finally, you will save the optimized image. Click the **Save** button.

9. In the **Save Optimized As** box, the chosen image appears next to the name of the file, the format chosen for optimization, JPG. Click the **Save** button to finish this exercise.

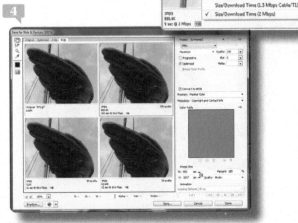

Saving optimization

PHOTOSHOP LETS YOU ADJUST the optimization settings of the images by using Save for Web & Devices to achieve an appropriate size value. Also, the program allows you to save any of these settings so you can use them quickly on other images at other times. The process of storing an optimized image begins once we have established the configuration saved for the web, which is in the Optimize menu.

1. In this exercise you will modify the image enhancement option and store the final configuration so that it can be used on other occasions. First, access the **Save for Web & Devices** box. Open the **File** menu and click **Save for Web & Devices** option

2. The box keeps the last changes made. In the format field, select **GIF**, 🔲 then click the check box to activate the **Interlaced** option. 🔲

3. Photoshop automatically optimizes the picture with the new parameters already selected. This option will gradually display the image in GIF format, should it be downloaded from

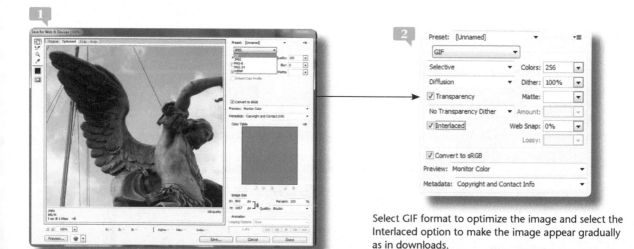

Select GIF format to optimize the image and select the Interlaced option to make the image appear gradually as in downloads.

the Internet. Now you will adjust the download speed. Dou-ble-click the **Web settings** field, type the value **25** and press **Return**.

4. Once you have optimized the image with the new parameters, you will save the current configuration. Click on the Options button to the right of the **Preset** section to display the **Opti-mize** menu and select **Save Settings**.

5. The **Save Optimization Settings** dialog box appears. The new settings should be included in the **Optimized Settings** folder, which by default is shown open in this window. In the **Name** field, type a descriptive name for the new setting and click **Save**.

6. Once you have saved the new configuration, apply one of the default settings to then see that you have saved it correctly. Display the **Preset** field menu and select **Gif Restrictive**.

7. Notice how the image changes. Reapply the saved setting. Display the Preset menu and select the one you have just stored.

8. As you can save custom settings, you can also remove them, by using the **Delete Settings** option from the **Optimize** menu. To finish this exercise, exit the **Save for Web & Devices** dialog box by clicking the **Cancel** button.

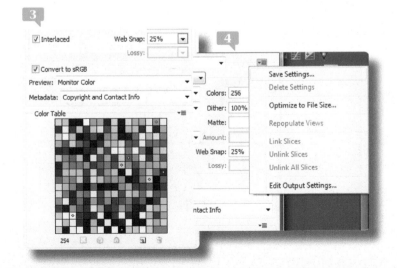

Check how the look of the image changes by applying different **preset optimization settings**.

Resizing an image when optimizing

FROM THE SAVE FOR WEB & DEVICES box you can resize an image to a specific pixel size or to a percentage of the original size. The change in dimensions of an image is carried out from the section size of the image, where, in addition to specifying the new dimensions in pixels or the percentage you want to resize the image with, you must also define the quality.

1. To begin, open the **File** menu and click **Save for Web & Devices** option.

2. The section **Image Size** shows the original image size in pixels. In the **W** and **H** fields you can insert new dimensions, also in pixels, or you can specify the percentage by which you want to resize the image. By default, the program maintains the proportions of pixel width and height.  Double-click the field **W**, which is relative to the width, enter the value **500**. Press **Return**.

3. In the **Quality** field you have to specify the resampling method to be used when resizing the image. The **Bicubic** option is

You can also access the dialog box Save for Web & Devices by pressing the key combination **Alt + Shift + Ctrl + S**.

generally the most appropriate when reducing the size of an image. Let's see what options you have. Click the arrow button in the **Quality** field and of the five resampling methods available, choose **Bicubic Smoother.**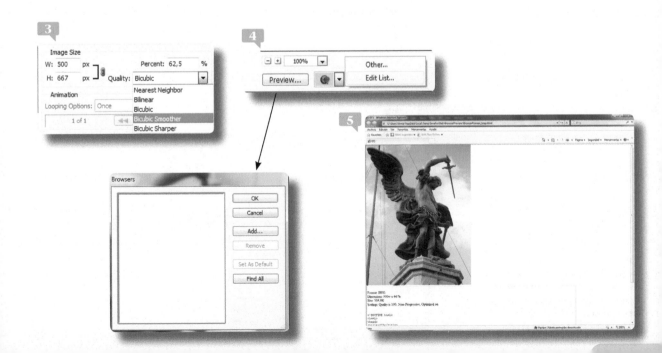

4. Optimized images can be previewed on any browser installed on your computer. To do this, simply click the **Preview** button at the bottom of the box **Save for Web & Devices.** To select another browser, you must use the **Other** option in the brower's selection menu, and to add, edit, or remove a browser, you should access the **Browsers** box using the **Edit List** from the same menu. To have the preview in your default browser, click the **Preview** button.

5. This opens the default browser on the computer and shows the image with a caption that tells you the type of image file, its pixel dimensions, file size, quality settings, and other data in HTML. Close the preview image by pressing the x on the title bar of the browser.

6. To finish this exercise, you will save the image with new dimensions. Click the **Save** button, type a new name for the image in the **Save Optimized As** dialog box and click the **Save** button to finish this exercise.

075

IMPORTANT

The **Quality** field refers to the interpolation method, usually the best results are obtained by reducing an image with the **Bicubic Sharper** option.

Quality:	Bicubic Sharper	▼

Nearest Neighbor
Bilinear
Bicubic
Bicubic Smoother
Bicubic Sharper

Establishing the output settings

TO ADJUST THE OUTPUT SETTINGS while optimizing images, you should access the Output Settings box, where you can edit the different sets of options. After defining the settings, you can save them anywhere on your computer to use whenever necessary.

1. The Output settings control the format of HTML files, the names of the files, and the management of background images. To begin, access the **Save for Web & Devices** box.

2. Click the icon to the right of **Preset** and choose **Edit Output Settings.**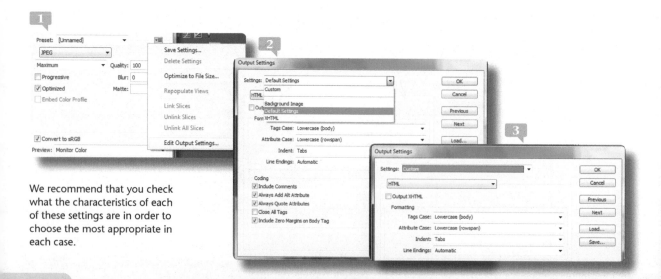

3. In the **Output Settings** dialog box you can set the options as you want them, and then store them so you can use them whenever you need them. To view the different predefined output options, press the arrow button in the **Settings** field.

4. As you can see the three default settings are **Default Settings**, **Background Image**, and XHTML. Click on the option **Custom** to select it.

5. The Output settings are divided into three sets: HTML, **Sectors Background**, and **Save Files.** You can switch from one to another using the **Previous** and **Next** buttons or by using the

We recommend that you check what the characteristics of each of these settings are in order to choose the most appropriate in each case.

076

menu under the **Settings** field. You begin by indicating in the settings that both HTML tags and attributes should be written in capital letters. Click on the arrow button in the **Tags Case** field then choose **Uppercase** (BODY).

6. Then press the arrow button in the **Attribute Case** field and choose **Uppercase** (ROWSPAN).

7. To see the output options for the background, press the arrow button next to the field and select the **Background** option.

8. In this section you indicate whether you want the Web page to show a picture or solid color as the background of the current image or if the optimized image is displayed as a segmented background. Click the **Background** option button then select **View Document As.**

9. Now, to display output options settings for **Saving Files,** click the **Next** button.

10. Click the check box option **Mac OS 9,** then **Filename Compatibility** and press the **Save** button.

11. As you can see in the **Save Output Settings**, the settings are stored in the default **Optimized Output Settings** folder, and have the IROS file extention. Type a file name and click **Save.**

12. Press the **OK** button on the **Output Settings** box, and finally, also exit the **Save for Web & Devices** by pressing the **Done** button.

Establish in the **Saving Files** section the compatibility of the file names.

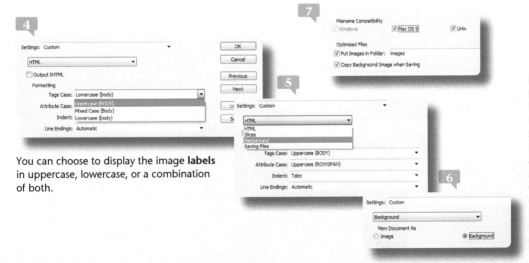

You can choose to display the image **labels** in uppercase, lowercase, or a combination of both.

If you leave the Image option in the **View Document As** section, you will be able to select an image that is stored on your computer to display it as the background of the optimized one.

Working with animated GIF

AN ANIMATED GIF IS A SIMPLE animation, and its creation presents no difficulty thanks to the Timeline panel. These animations are very useful for creating banner ads for a website. Animated GIFs are composed of two or more frames, which are controlled from the said panel.

1. Create a new blank canvas 300 pixels wide by 100 high and with a transparent background. 🔲

2. The simple animation you create will consist of a square that moves from one side of the canvas to the other. You start by drawing the square at the starting point of the trajectory. Click the arrowhead of the **Custom Shape Tool** and select the **Rounded Rectangle Tool**. 🔲

3. From the **Options Bar**, set it as a fixed size of 55px perfect. (If you forget how to do it, please review exercises 68 and 69.) 🔲

4. Remember that this will be the starting point of a short path. Place the square on the bottom right of the canvas. 🔲

5. Pull down the **Window** menu and select **Timeline**.

6. The **Timeline** panel appears, ready to create the animation. To do this, press the arrow button to the right of the command

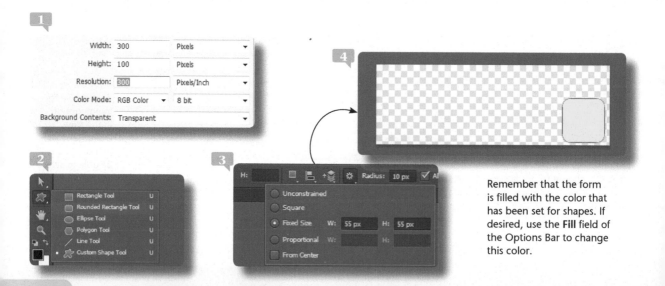

Remember that the form is filled with the color that has been set for shapes. If desired, use the **Fill** field of the Options Bar to change this color.

077

Create Video Timeline, select **Create Frame Animation** and then click on the rename button.

7. You will continue the exercise by adding a second frame. Click the button **Duplicate selected frames**, which is represented by a small sheet of paper.

8. It creates a new frame with the same object as above. To create a basic animation, you just have to change the location of the object within one of the two frames. Choose the **Move Tool** in the Tools pane and drag the square to place it at the opposite end of the canvas.

9. Now the frames have the same object but in different locations. Before playing the animation, change the delay time of the frames. Click the time that appears below the second frame and select **1.0**.

10. Click on the time that now appears below the first frame and select the same time.

11. To test the effect of the animation, click the **Play animation** command, represented by an arrow pointing to the right at the bottom of the panel.

In the **Select Looping Options** field, the **Once** option is enabled by default, the animation plays once and stops only when it ends. Otherwise, stop it manually by pressing the **Stop** button, the only activated option in the **Timeline** panel.

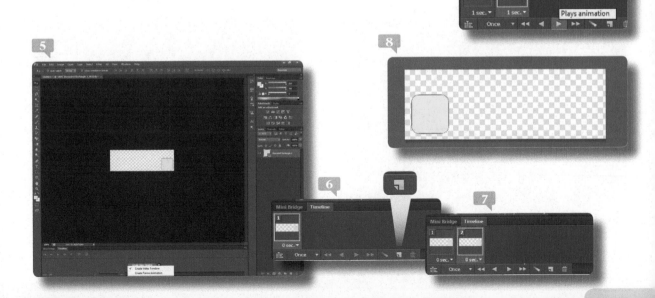

Adjusting the opacity of layers for animation

IMPORTANT

You can specify the number of times you want to play the animation using the menu options on the left of the playback controls in the **Timeline** panel. If you choose **Other**, you can define the number of repetitions yourself.

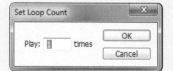

ANOTHER WAY TO ANIMATE AN OBJECT in Photoshop is to create frames and then adjust the opacity of a layer. To do this you need to have at least two frames. One will set the minimum level of visibility and the second, the degree of maximum visibility. By interleaving frames of animation, Photoshop automatically creates frames that are necessary for the gradual appearance of the object.

1. In this exercise you will create an animation in which an object gradually appears over five frames. You can use file **078.psd**, which you will find in the download area of our website. Start by duplicating the existing single frame by clicking the icon **Duplicate selected frames** in the **Timeline** panel. 🗨1

2. Note that in our sample file, the ball is on a separate layer. It will be the opacity of that layer in the first frame that you will modify to create the animation. Select the first frame, activate Layer 1 in the **Layers** panel and set the opacity to 0%. 🗨2

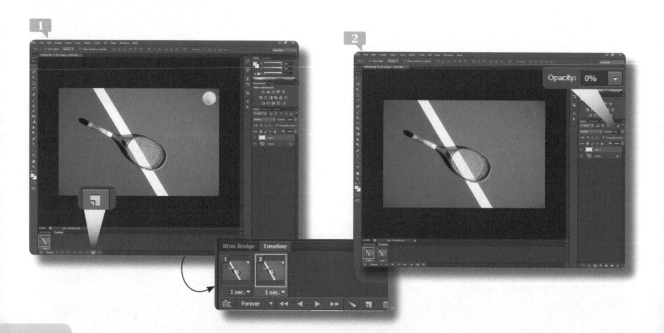

078

3. The visibility of the ball on this frame is now zero, whereas in the second frame it is 100%. Select the second frame and with the **Move Tool**, move the ball to put it on the racket. 3

4. For Photoshop to automatically create the sequence of frames showing the object gradually, click the command **Tweens animation frames**, the fifth button in the **Timeline** panel. 4

5. In the **Tween** box you can provide some of the features of the sequence of frames that you are about to add to your animation. Keep **All Layers** enabled 5 so that the frames appear in all layers. Press **OK** to confirm.

6. Five frames are automatically added so that with the gradual appearance of the object, the animation now consists of 7 frames. 6 Press the **Play animation** button to see the final result.

7. If you want it so that the ball does not go away entirely, you can delete the first frame, where the layer opacity is 0%. To do this, select it and click **Delete selected frames**, whose icon shows a trash can. 7

8. Confirm that you want to remove the frame, 8 then play back the animation to see the final result.

By default, the program adds five frames, but you can enlarge or reduce this number and the items to be displayed during the animation.

Optimizing interactive images

AN ANIMATION MADE WITH PHOTOSHOP can only be optimized in GIF format, since this is the only format that allows moving images on the Internet. Optimizing an animation can be done by optimizing all the frames and component parts or by optimizing animations by a special screening technique, so that images that have already been shown do not recur, or that a previously used animation is reproduced.

1. To begin, click the icon with an arrow on the far right of the **Timeline** panel and choose **Optimize Animation.** ▇

2. The **Optimize Animation** box appears with two options, **Bounding Box** and **Redundant Pixel Removal,** keep both selected. The first allows you to crop each frame in the area that has changed from the above window, while the second allows you to make transparent all pixels of a picture that has not changed with respect to the above window. Keep them activated and click **OK.** ▇

3. Once the animation is optimized, save it as a GIF format image. Pull down the **File** menu and click on **Save for Web & Devices**.

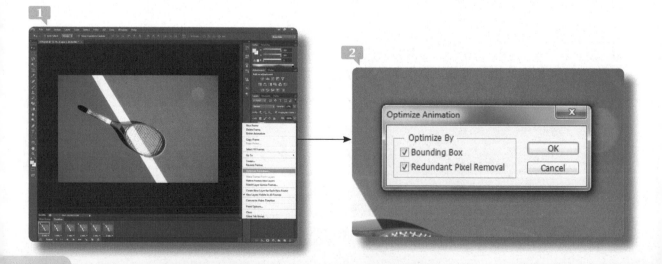

4. Click the arrow button in the **Format** field, showing the JPEG format, and select **GIF**.

5. Then, in the **Color Reduction Algorithm**, which is situated below the format options, choose **Selective**.

6. The information about the animation is now in the Status Bar. In this case, Photoshop indicates the size and time of download. You will now change the repeat options. Click the arrow button on the **Looping Options** field and select **Other**.

7. In the **Play** field in the **Set Loop Count** box, enter a value of **2** and click **OK**.

8. Thus, the animation will play twice when inserted into a web page. Get a preview in your web browser to check the result. Click the **Preview** button at the bottom of the window.

9. This opens the default browser showing the animation. When the animation has played twice as was expected, close the browser.

10. Click the **Save** button, type a name in the **Save Optimized As** dialog box and click the **Save** button.

You now have an animated gif that can be inserted into a website designer, for example, Dreamweaver.

The animations that will be embedded in a web page should be optimized in GIF format.

Creating rollovers

IMPORTANT

You can also create rollover effects by changing the position and opacity of the layers, adjusting tones and colors, applying filters, and creating color overlays, shadows, glows, embossing, etc. for each state of a button. Rollover effects can be saved in image formats compatible with the web and in an optimized file size from the **Save for Web & Devices** dialog box.

ROLLOVERS ARE NORMALLY INTENDED to be included in a website and are objects that act as buttons that change appearance depending on position of the mouse over them.

1. Start this exercise with a blank canvas of 150 pixels square, where you should insert an ellipse of 100 dots wide by 50 high by using the **Ellipse Tool.** To display the **Styles** pane, click the corresponding tab in the second group of panels.

2. You will replace the default styles that appear in this panel for buttons. Click the small icon to the right of the panel, which displays the menu and, then select the above category.

3. To replace the current styles for buttons, press the **OK** button in the dialog box that appears.

4. To create the first state of the button, you will apply the style **Beveled Mouseover** to the ellipse and store the resulting image as a separate document. Click on the fourth panel that shows the **Styles,** which correspond to that style.

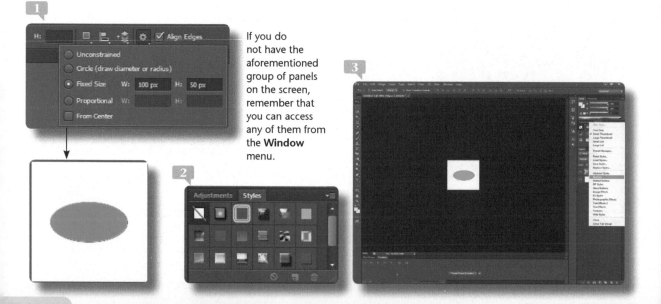

If you do not have the aforementioned group of panels on the screen, remember that you can access any of them from the **Window** menu.

5. The effect is automatically applied. To display the **History** panel, click the first icon in the palette of coupled elements, then, to create a new document from the current state, click the first icon in the panel. **5**

6. Save the new file from the **File** menu with a descriptive name and then close it by pressing the x on the tab to return to the original document.

7. The next step is to apply a tight button style to the object and to also save the resulting image. To eliminate the mouseover effect, drag the letters **fx** to the trash at the bottom of the **Layers** panel. **6**

8. Click on the fifth icon on the **Styles** palette, for the **Beveled Mousedown** button. **7**

9. After applying the style, from the **History** panel create a new document from the image and save it with a descriptive name for the button state.

10. Now you have two rollover images you can place in a program to create websites, such as Dreamweaver. To finish this exercise, close the current image by clicking on the x on its tab.

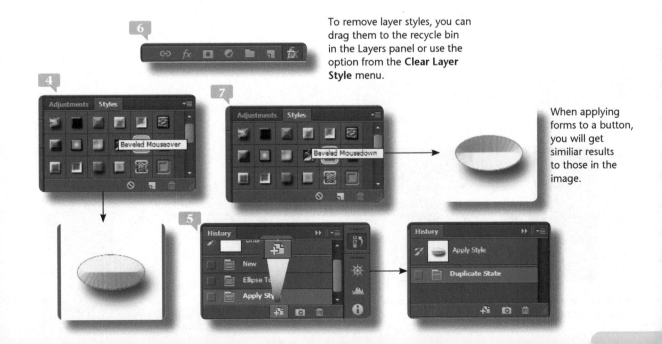

To remove layer styles, you can drag them to the recycle bin in the Layers panel or use the option from the **Clear Layer Style** menu.

When applying forms to a button, you will get similiar results to those in the image.

Adjusting Tests

KEEPING THE ORIGINAL COLORS on a hard copy is very important. Therefore, you should usually do some color tests before printing a document. In this way, you can test the document directly in the monitor application, which will show a preview on the screen of how the document will look on specific devices.

1. In this exercise you will see how to check the intensity of colors as they would be printed in a document. Open the **View** menu, click the **Proof Setup** command and choose **Working Cyan Plate.** 1

2. This option lets you test the application of cyan in CMYK using specific ink colors. Again, open the **View** menu, click the **Proof Setup** command and choose **Working Yellow Plate.** 2

3. The shaded tones are those belonging to the yellow range. Next, you will do a new color test. Open the **View** menu, click the **Proof Setup** command and choose **Working CMY Plate.** 3

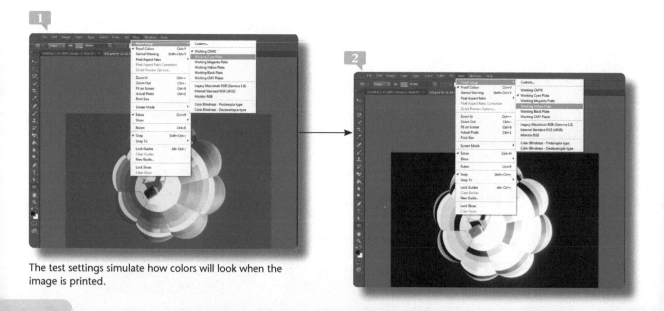

The test settings simulate how colors will look when the image is printed.

081

4. The plates show the colors of CMYK inks using specific CMYK working space assets. This option, in turn, shows you the main colors of the drawing, but not the original colors. Next, you will see the RGB colors of Windows. Open the **View** menu, click on the **Proof Setup** command and choose **Standard Internet RGB (sRGB).**

5. This option lets you test the application of colors in an RGB document for the color space of the monitor as a demonstration of the test profile. That is, it shows all the colors that Windows and the monitor can show, which in this case, are the original colors. Finally, once again, open the **View** menu, click the **Proof Setup** command and select **Custom.**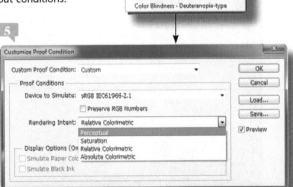

6. In the **Customize Proof Condition** box you can establish a specific ICC profile and modify or maintain the monitor's color settings. This time, you will only modify the color values. Deselect the **Preserve RGB Numbers** option.

7. Click the arrow button in the **Rendering Intent** field and select **Perceptual.**

8. This option allows us to maintain the visual relationship between the colors, so that the human eye perceives them as natural although in printing they may vary. Click **OK** to apply the new profile.

IMPORTANT

Through the **Proof Setup** menu options, you can customize the color test using specific color profiles, to see the CMYK workspace with the cyan, magenta, yellow, and black plates, and even see the RGB colors of Windows and Macintosh.

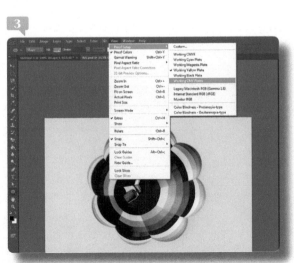

The choice of test settings box opens the **Customize Prof Condition** box, where you can create a custom configuration for specific output conditions.

Preparing color channels for printing

BEFORE PRINTING A DOCUMENT FROM PHOTOSHOP, you should know that each image consists of multiple color channels, which vary depending on whether the images are RGB or CMYK. RGB images are composed of three channels (red, green, and blue) and CMYK are composed of four channels (cyan, magenta, yellow, and black). The channels can be displayed in the Channels panel.

1. To perform this exercise you can use any image you have stored on your computer or, if desired, file **082.jpg,** which you can find in the download area of our website. First, create a duplicate of the image. Pull down the **Image** menu and select **Duplicate.**

2. In the **Duplicate Image** dialog box, keep the name the program assigns to the new document and press **OK** to create it. ▬

3. You will make changes to this copy and compare it with the original image. To check the differences between the two im-

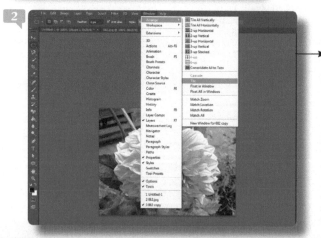

ages that you will apply the changes to, you will display them next to each other. Open the **Window** menu, click the **Arrange** option and then click the **Tile** command.

4. The first change you will make is to establish a new color palette for the copied file. Pull down the **Image** menu, click the **Mode** command and in the submenu that appears, select the **CMYK Color** option.

5. A dialog box warns us that the image will now have a specific color profile that can be modified using the **Convert To Profile** option from the **Edit** menu. Click the **OK** button.

6. A slight difference between the two images can now be seen. This is because the colors of both documents are the same, but the duplicate of the original image now has the CMYK channel—a palette of four colors. To view all four channels of the duplicated image, click the tab of the **Channels** panel.

7. Effectively, this panel shows a first channel with the name **CMYK** and then four channels corresponding to the colors cyan, magenta, yellow, and black. By contrast, the original image contains only red, green, and blue. Click the tab of the original document and see the channels in the corresponding panel to finish this simple exercise.

IMPORTANT

The command **Arrange** in the **Window** menu has been enhanced in this version of Photoshop, and now has ten ways to organize the open documents in the workspace.

The first channel will show the union of all colors and identified with the corresponding name (RGB or CMYK), while the rest of the colors are displayed on the active image.

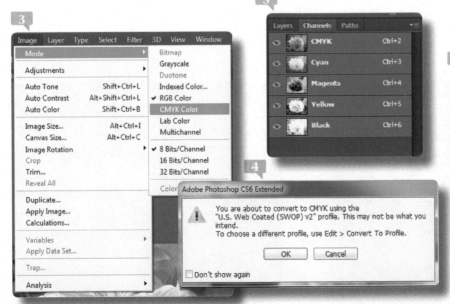

Manipulating image channels

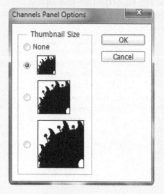
THE COLOR VALUES OF AN IMAGE change depending on their color mode. So when we convert an image from one color mode to another, their values are also modified. Values are adjusted depending on the mode of the original image and the mode it will be changed to. However, not all color modes can be converted easily.

1. In this exercise you will see how to manipulate the color channels of images **082** and **082 copy,** which you used in the previous lesson. The first is an RGB image composed of three channels: red, green, and blue. In the **Channels** panel, turn off the **Red** channel by clicking on the appropriate visibility box.

2. Hiding the red channel shows the complete picture with **blue** as the predominant color. Reactivate the same channel.

3. Then, turn off the **Blue** channel, and now the predominant color is yellow. Now also deactivate the **Red** channel.

4. The image is now displayed in black and white. To return all the original colors to the image, click the box for **RGB** channel visibility.

5. Now you will manipulate the colors of the mirror image,

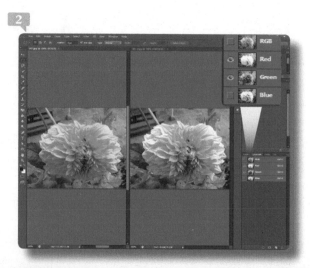

which you converted to CMYK mode in the previous exercise. Click the tab for that image.

6. In the **Channels** panel, click the visibility box for the **Magenta** channel and then the **Yellow** channel to hide them.

7. Now, the only existing color in the image is blue, since it is the only one that remains active, as well as black. Click the channel visibility box **Black** and, after checking that the image loses all color, click the **Magenta** channel to re-display it.

8. Now the image is shown again in two colors: cyan and magenta. Click the **yellow** channel visibility box to recover it and as you will see that the lack of black causes some areas to not be fully defined, activate the **Black** channel to redisplay all colors.

9. Finally, convert the CMYK image to a multichannel image. Pull down the **Image** menu, click in the **Mode** command, and from the submenu, select **Multichannel.**

10. In the **Channels** panel you now have four colors: cyan, magenta, yellow, and black. To hide the **Cyan** channel, click on its visibility box. Then do the same to hide the **Yellow** channel.

11. Click on the visibility box for yellow, and finish the exercise by clicking on the channel visibility box.

IMPORTANT

Multichannel mode uses 256 levels of gray in each channel and is often used for printing special images.

Creating new channels

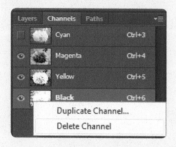
ALL COLOR CHANNELS, INCLUDING RGB AND CMYK and Multichannel, can be duplicated or manipulated. In general, channels are often duplicated and then changed later. To duplicate the channels of an image, it must be RGB, CMYK, or Multichannel, but never Bitmap.

1. With your duplicate document in the foreground (you can keep working with files **082** and **082 copy**), click on the **Yellow** channel in the **Channels** panel to select it.

2. Click the options button of the panel and choose **Duplicate Channel.** 🔲

3. The **Duplicate Channel** box displays the name assigned by Photoshop for the new element and the one you want to include it in. Click **OK** to continue. 🔲

4. A new channel in the **Channels** panel appears. It is called **Yellow copy** and has the same features as the Yellow channel. 🔲 To modify the properties, double-click it.

5. The **Spot Channel Options** box contains the characteristics of the selected channel. First, rename the channel. In the **Name** field, type **Green**. 🔲

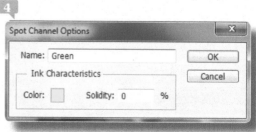

Instead of double-clicking on the channel you want to edit, you can also access the Panel Options menu and choose **Channel Options**.

6. To continue the exercise, you will choose the color that you specified for the channel so that it is shown in the image too. Click the **Color** box.

7. In the **Color Picker** box, select a green tone and press the **OK** button.

8. Now you will establish the degree of visibility of the color. In the **Solidity** field, enter the value **50** and press **OK** to apply the new values to the color channel.

9. Click on the visibility boxes of the **Magenta** and **Yellow** channel to hide them. Then click the **Green** channel visibility checkbox.

10. Note that there should always be one active channel. Click the channel visibility box to hide **Black**.

11. Now only the new channel is visible, so the image appears in black and white. Display the other colors.

12. Note that, even by showing all the colors of the channels, green continues to be the dominant color. This is because all the channels have a solid percentage of 0%, while the new channel that you created has a strength of 50%. You will reduce this percentage. Double-click on the **Green** channel.

13. In the **Spot Channel Options** box, enter the value **1** in the **Solidity** field to reduce the visibility of the new channel, then press **OK** to apply the changes.

Printing with preview

THE PRINT COMMAND FROM THE FILE MENU allows you to set the image size for the page where it will be printed, and offers the possibility of adding a border or specifying a background color for the page. The Print Settings box of Photoshop has a preview page where you can see a preview before you print the image. It is also where you make any changes to the settings.

1. Pull down the **File** menu and select **Print.** 🔲

2. The **Photoshop Print Settings** box appears, which has been extensively renovated in the CS6 version of the program. First of all, you will increase the size of the image. Go to the **Position** and **Size** section and in the **Scale** field, enter **120.** 🔲

3. In addition to the scale, it is also possible to change the size of the image. Double-click in the **Height** field and insert a value of **15.**

4. Now show the contents of the **Functions** section. 🔲

5. All the commands needed to change the image format are listed. In this case, click the **Background** button. 🔲

The values **Scale, Height,** and **Width** are related, so that by modifying one of them, the others automatically change proportionally to keep the image from distorting.

085

6. In the **Color Picker (Print Background Color)** box, select the color you want and press **OK** to apply it as the background.

7. To highlight the image a bit more with this background, apply a small border around it. Click the **Border** button.

8. In the **Width** field of the dialog box, enter the value **1** and click **OK** to confirm.

9. You can continue to make changes to the settings from the preview box. To continue the exercise, you will apply some editing marks. To do this, display the contents of the **Printing Marks** section. Click the check box option **Registration Marks**.

10. Registration marks include a series of marks outside the boundaries of the image that are used to align color separations. Uncheck that option and activate the **Corner Crop Marks.**

11. The corner marks are guides used for physically cutting the pages later. Disable this option and select **Center Crop Marks.**

12. Center crop marks, like the corner crop marks, are a guide for cutting the final page. Once you set the formatting options, press the **Print** button to print the document.

Creating and printing duotones

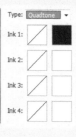
PHOTOSHOP CAN CONVERT images to duotones, from an image in Grayscale mode, so as to increase the tonal richness. Photoshop duotones are treated as grayscale images in a single channel of 8 bits.

1. To perform this exercise you can use the example image **086.jpg** which can be found as always on our website. The first step you must take to create a duotone image is to convert the image to grayscale. Open the **Image** menu, click on the **Mode** command and choose **Grayscale**. 🗨1

2. A warning box appears to inform you that the program will remove all the color information. Press the **OK** button. 🗨2

3. Once you have the image in grayscale mode, you must convert it to the Duotone mode. Re-open the **Image** menu, click on the command **Mode** and choose **Duotone**.

4. The **Duotone Options** dialog box displays the type of **Monotone** enabled by default. To change this, click the arrow button in the **Type** field and select **Duotone**. 🗨3

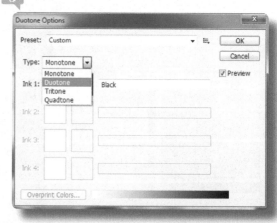

When converting a duotone image, there is no direct access to the **individual channels** of the image. They should be handled by the curves in the Duotone Options box.

086

5. Photoshop displays black and white by default. Let's change them. Click the white color box of **Ink 2**.

6. The **Color Picker (Ink 2 Color)** dialog box appears. To select a color, Photoshop has a complete catalog of Pantone colors available, which includes a wide variety of tones. In the color bar, see all the shades of blue, select one of the samples shown in the graph on the left and click **OK** to apply it.

7. Note that the image now combines the two active colors in the **Duotone Options** dialog box. Type a name in the edit field for the second ink and then press **OK** to apply changes.

8. After converting the image, you will see how it prints. Open the menu **File** and click on the **Print** command.

9. In the **Photoshop Print Settings** dialog box, display the **Color Handling** field of the **Color Management** section. For a better end result, select **Separations**.

10. As a final print setting, check the **Scale To Half Fit** option of the **Position and Size** section to fit on the page and press the **Print** button.

11. To finish the exercise, keep a copy of the modified image in the Duotone mode.

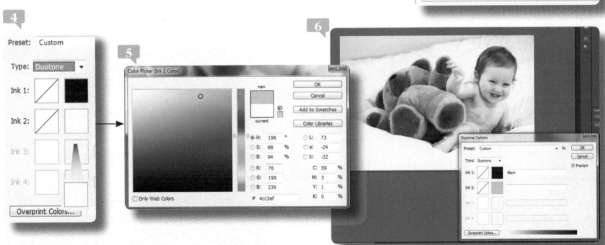

For fully saturated colors, choose inks in descending order, that is, darker above and lighter below.

It should be noted that both the order of printing inks and screen angles influence the final effect.

Importing 3D objects

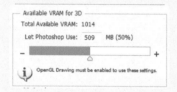

WITH PHOTOSHOP YOU CAN IMPORT files in three dimensions. Thanks to the support Photoshop offers 3D files, you can work with common 3D file formats: .u3d, .3ds, .Obj, .Kmz, and Collada, as well as, 3D design programs like Adobe Acrobat 3D, 3D Studio Max, Alias, Maya, and Google Earth. When you import 3D objects into Photoshop, the program places them in a separate 3D layer and allows you to make changes in scale, lighting, at the nodes of interpretation, and so on, as well as moving the models with the 3D tools.

1. For this exercise, you will need a 3D image of one of the formats indicated in the introduction that you have stored on your computer. You can use, if you want, file **087.3ds,** which can be found on our website. Open the **3D** menu and click on the option **New 3D Layer from File.** 🔲

2. Locate and select the file you will use and click **Open.** 🔲

3. New to this version of Photoshop is a warning box that asks for confirmation before switching to a 3D workspace. Click the **Yes** button to access this new 3D workspace. 🔲

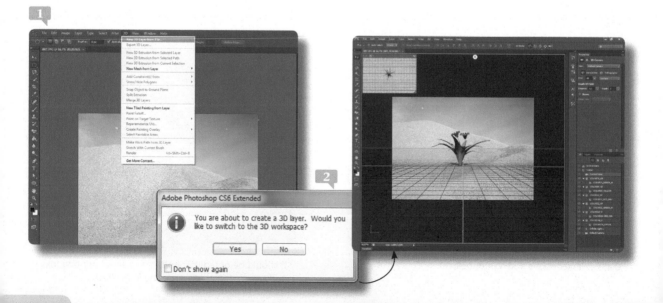

4. A layer is automatically added to the document you were working with. The cube-shaped icon that appears on the thumbnail in the **Layers** panel indicates that it is a 3D layer. Thanks to the **3D** panel, you can edit and manipulate 3D images without dialog boxes. As an example, you will modify the illumination of the image. Click the **Infinite Light 1** element. 3

5. Notice how the workspace adapts the interface to display the image directly on the regulators to change the position, orientation, and intensity of light. 4 To change the light intensity, position the pointer over the central regulator adjustment, and by dragging, increase or decrease the intensity. 5

6. In the same way as the intensity changes, you can also change the position of the lights, the scene materials, etc., with the icons of this panel. You will see how to use some of the 3D tools in future exercises. Click on the **Background** layer in the **Layers** panel to exit 3D editing.

7. You will now save this file with 3D layer in the Photoshop format. Open the **File menu,** click on **Save** and, after finding that that Photoshop PSD PDD is selected in the Format field, click **Save.**

087

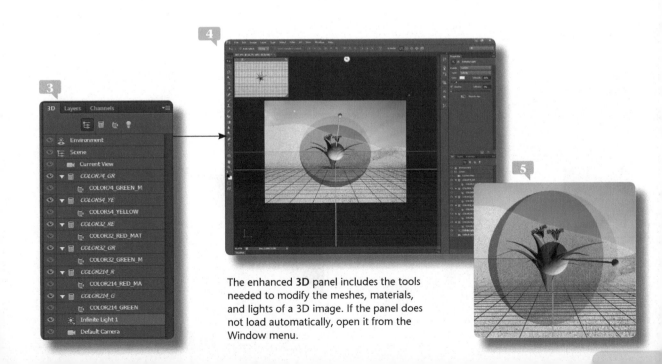

The enhanced **3D** panel includes the tools needed to modify the meshes, materials, and lights of a 3D image. If the panel does not load automatically, open it from the Window menu.

Converting 2D images into 3D images

PHOTOSHOP ALLOWS YOU TO CONVERT 2D OBJECTS into 3D objects. You can apply 2D image wraps around common 3D shapes such as pyramids, donuts, spheres, spherical panoramas, etc., with easily applied preset settings. You can even convert gradient maps into 3D objects.

1. Start this exercise with a transparent canvas that is 400 by 400 pixels. On this canvas you will create a gradient map that will later become a 3D object. Click the arrowhead of the **Paint Bucket Tool** and select the **Gradient Tool**.

2. Click the arrow button of the gradient sample in the **Options Bar** and choose by double-clicking one of the gradient samples available.

3. To apply a linear gradient to the bottom of the document, click and drag from one point to another.

4. After you have created a gradient map in the **3D** panel, select the **Mesh From Preset** option. Display the next field and select, for example, **Soda.**

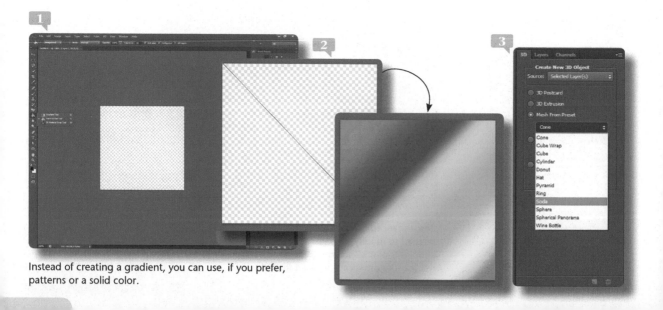

Instead of creating a gradient, you can use, if you prefer, patterns or a solid color.

5. Press the **Create** button and check in the **Layers** pane that the bottom layer has become a 3D layer and that the editing options of 3D objects have already appeared in the **3D panel**. 4

6. Choose the **Move Tool** to load in the Options Bar dimensional transformation tools, select the first option, **Rotate the 3D object** and drag the image to verify that the gradient map has been distributed as a label on the chosen shape. 5

7. Exit the new 3D interface by clicking the selection tool and saving the image.

8. Now open a JPG image in Photoshop of a landscape that you have stored on your computer, display the **3D menu**, click the **New Mesh From Layer** command, choose the **Mesh Preset** screen and select, for example, **Sphere**. 6

9. Use the 3D rotation and displacement tools to check the effect.

10. Finally, you will export the 3D layer you're working with to one of the available formats. Open the **3D** menu and click on **Export 3D Layer**. 7

11. Press the arrow button on the **Format** field, choose **Google Earth**, and click the **Save** button.

12. To finish the exercise, keep the 3D export options that are displayed in the dialog box and click **OK**.

IMPORTANT

With enhanced editing tools for 3D objects you can create sophisticated **3D animation** from the Timeline panel controlling the movement of an object, the camera placement, lighting effects, texture mapping, etc.

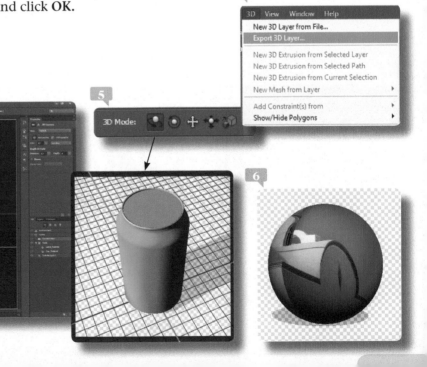

Getting to know the new 3D tools

IN THE PREVIOUS EXERCISES YOU HAVE SEEN the changes to the interface to activate 3D work. In this activity you will check the operation of two new tools, the 3D Material Dropper and 3D Material Eyedropper, the first is included in the group headed by the paint bucket, while the second is in the dropper group.

1. To perform this exercise, use both of the 3D documents you created in the previous exercise, which should still be open. If they aren't available, you you can always use images **089_1.psd**, and **089_2.psd,** which are available on our website. We begin by learning how the new **3D Material Drop Tool** works. Go to the first image, the can. Open the **Gradient Tool** and select the option **3D Material Drop Tool.** 🔲

2. In the Options Bar you can verify that you are not currently working with any 3D material. 🔲 Display the sample box, and after viewing the materials available, double-click the first one to select it. 🔲

3. The selected material is loaded into the program, ready to be applied, check that its name is now shown in the Options Bar.

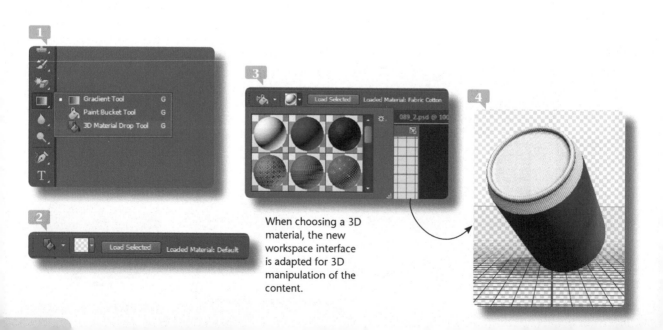

When choosing a 3D material, the new workspace interface is adapted for 3D manipulation of the content.

To assign the new material to the top of our soda can click on this part of the image and observe the result. [4]

4. As you can see, the selected material is applied to the designated portion, while respecting the label. You will now select just the material of the label and apply it to the sphere in the second document. To do this, in the **3D** panel, select the material **Label_Material** and in the Options Bar, click the **Load Selected** button. [5]

5. Note the change in the samples field of this bar and in the text of the currently loaded material. Put the second image, the sphere, in the foreground and check that the label material remains loaded. Click on the object.

6. As you can see, the field now shows the graduated material. [6] The second tool that we will describe in this exercise works in a similar way to the first, the **3D Material Eyedropper Tool**. Display the **Eyedropper Tool** in the Tools pane, which occupies the sixth position, and then select the aforementioned new tool. [7]

7. This tool works like the conventional dropper, that is, in combination with the fill tool or paint bucket. Return to the first document, take a sample of the material from the top of the can with a click, return to the document area and, after selecting **3D Material Drop**, fill the area with the sampled material. [8]

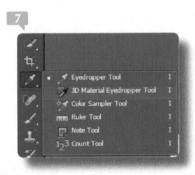

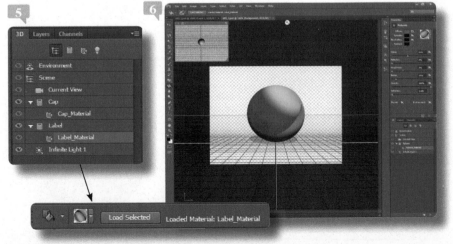

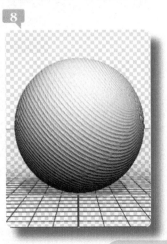

More 3D objects and materials

PHOTOSHOP HAS A REDUCED CATALOG OF MATERIALS that you can expand by downloading extra elements from the Web. To facilitate this, the 3D menu has a link that will lead you to the website where you can download these elements. You should take into account, however, that the downloading 3D objects sometimes involve an additional payment.

1. Before we start, we want to inform you that the contents of this exercise may require you to pay for the downloads, which may be subject to change over time due to constant updating. To begin, pull down the **3D** menu and click on the **Get More Content** command.

2. This opens the default Web browser on your computer, from where you can easily download both 3D models and material. As noted in the introduction, it is possible that in some cases, providers of 3D models may require you to purchase the models. Investigate the options, and when you find a pattern that interests you, follow the steps to download it.

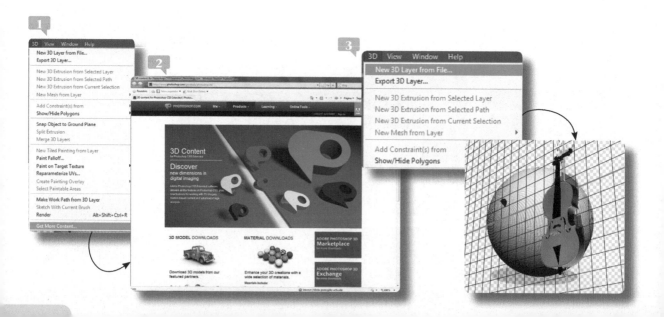

3. Once downloaded and saved on your computer, you can import it using the Photoshop workspace (**3D/New 3D Layer from File**).

4. Let's see how to get more materials in this way. Download and save the resource kit to your computer by following the usual steps.

5. Photoshop has a command to load new material in a palette of materials that are already available. In this case, select the **3D Material Drop Tool** in the Tools pane and in the Options Bar, click on the field of material samples.

6. In the pane that contains the materials available, click on the round icon located on the right side of it and click on the **Load Materials** command.

7. It opens a dialog box that allows you to access the website from where you have downloaded the new materials. Press the **Go** button, or access the folder where you saved the elements in question. In this case, click on the **OK** button.

8. In the **Load** dialog box, locate the folder of downloaded materials, choose one of the categories of materials and press the **Load** button to load the materials in this category.

9. Finally, check that the new material appears in the following panel of samples by default. To apply one of them to the 3D object in your image, select it with a double-click and then click on the object.

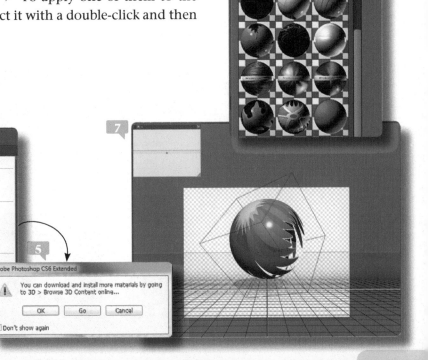

Creating actions

PHOTOSHOP ALLOWS YOU TO AUTOMIZE actions to modify, create, or delete images quickly and easily. An action is a set of commands that run on a file or a batch of files. Photoshop offers users a number of preset actions in the Actions panel.

1. In this exercise you will create a new action that consists of several steps. To begin, pull down the **Window** menu, click on the **Actions** command and in the panel of the same name, click the fifth icon, **Create new action.**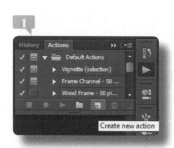

2. In the **Name** of the **New Action** box, type the word **Duotone.**

3. Then assign a function key to the new action. Open the menu of the **Function key** and select **F2.**

4. Press **Record** to begin storing the actions.

5. Note that in **Actions** pane displays the name of the new action next to the assigned function key. To begin creating the steps for this action, open the **Image** menu, click on the **Mode** command and choose **Grayscale.**

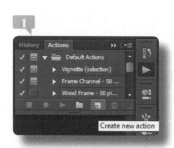

You can also activate the **Actions** panel with the key combination Alt + F9.

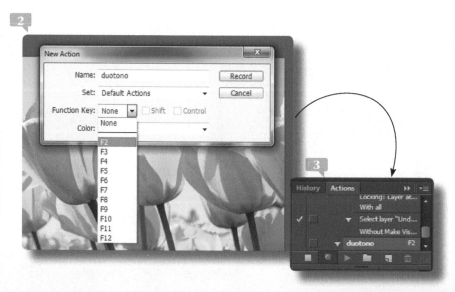

6. Photoshop warns you that you will lose the current colors. Click **Discard** to continue the process.

7. Then display the **Image** menu again, choose the **Mode** command and select **Duotone**.

8. A **Duotone Options** dialog box appears, which you have worked with in a previous lesson. Choose the duotone colors you want and press the **OK** button.

9. Press the **Stop playing/recording** command, the first icon in the **Actions** panel.

10. After creating the action, you will test a new image using the assigned function key. Open any image that is stored on your computer and that can be retouched.

11. Click on the action with the name **Duotone** in the **Actions** panel and press **F2.**

12. The image has taken on the appearance of the action you have created.  Recorded actions can be modified and even eliminated. Select the last action recorded with the name **Convert Mode** and press the trash icon in the **Actions** panel.

13. In the confirmation dialog box, click **OK.**

14. The **Duotone** action now covers only the first step in this case: converting the image to the grayscale mode. Press the **F2** key to run the action and check the result.

Working with batches

ALL ACTIONS DESCRIBED in previous lessons can be applied jointly to a group of images or a file folder or subfolders by using the Batch option. In the Batch dialog box, specify the group that the image belongs to: the action, and the folder or drive where the images or files you want to modify are. You can even access an external drive such as a digital camera or scanner, and implement an action.

IMPORTANT

You can specify in the **Destination** section where you want the processed files to be stored. If you leave the None option selected, the files remain open in Photoshop until you store them.

1. In this exercise you will learn to apply the action taken in the previous exercise to a group of images. To do this, create a folder with several pictures. Begin the exercise by pulling down the **File** menu, click the **Automate** command and then select **Batch**.

2. In the **Batch** menu you must select the group that contains the action you wish to apply. What you want to do is to convert the image color mode to duotone, an action, which as you will remember, you created in the **Default Actions** group. In the **Set** field select that same group while in the **Action** field, select **Duotone**.

The **Batch** command in the **File** menu option runs a selected action in the **Batch** file folder.

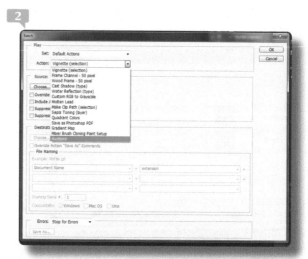

The **Batch** box menus show the groups and the actions that are included in the **Actions** pane. Select those which are going to be applied to the batch.

3. Remember that this action was modified in the previous exercise, so that it will only perform the first step: converting the image to black and white. Next, choose the image source. If you decide to use a series of images taken with a digital camera or captured from a scanner, you must choose **Import** in this field, and then the indicated steps. In this case, keep the **Folder** option in the **Source** field and press **Choose.**

4. In the **Search Folder** box, locate and select your folder and then press **OK.**

5. Once you have determined the action you want to apply and where the pictures you want to convert are, click **OK** to confirm the process.

6. By confirming the process, one by one all the images in the selected folder are automatically opened, and the system implements each action indicated. To finish, you will close the images manually while saving the changes. Keep in mind, that you can also specify in the **Batch** box if you want to store the resulting conversed images, and the place where to store them automatically. Open the **File** menu and choose **Close All.**

7. Confirm that you want to save the changes by pressing the **Yes** box on the screen and keeping the options as they appear by default in the **JPEG Options** dialog box. Repeat this with the other images.

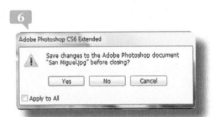

Importing a PDF image

IMPORTANT

By default, thumbnails are displayed small, but you can change that in the **Thumbnail Size** field.

THE PDF FORMAT ALLOWS YOU TO STORE and combine in a single file vector data and images with various formats (BMP, JPEG, GIF, etc), as well as incorporating search and navigation functions. It is possible that these files are divided into several pages and images. So when you want to use some of them in Photoshop, you must open or import files with a PDF extension, depending on the function or the images you wish to load. It is not the same as importing a PDF file where you get only the pictures it contains.

1. For this exercise, use the PDF file **093.pdf,** which you will find in the download area of our website. Once you've copied it into your Documents folder, open the **File** menu, choose **Open,** locate it then select it, and click **Open** to start the import process. 🔳

2. The **Import PDF** box appears. To test for differences between import pages or images from a document of this type, you will carry out the process twice. With the **Pages** option activated in the **Select** field, select the first page and then press the **OK** button. 🔳

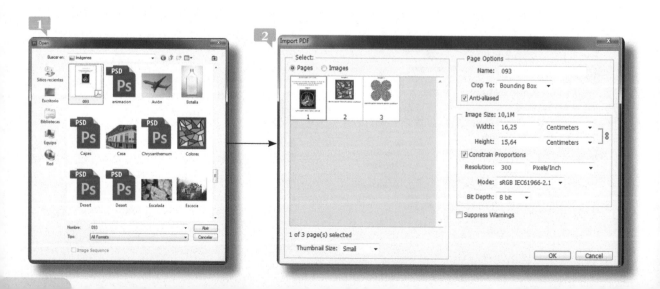

093

3. As you can see in the **Layers** panel, the selected page opens in a single layer with a transparent background. 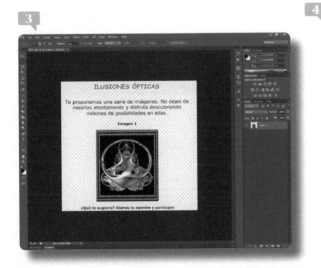 If you had chosen the other pages of the document, the program would open in separate canvases, each with a single layer. Let's see what happens when you import only the images. Open the **File** menu and click the **Open** command.

4. In the **Open** dialog box, select the PDF file and click **Open.**

5. In the **Select** section, activate the **Images** option.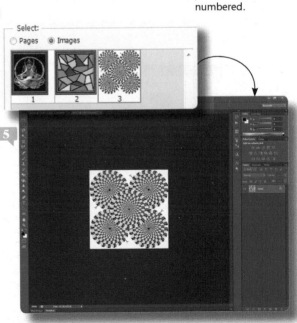

6. Notice the change that has occurred in the box. On the side, the thumbnails now show only the images contained in each of the pages. On the other side, the options for the **Page Options** appear deactivated. Select one of the images and click **OK** to import it into Photoshop.

7. You have now obtained a new document. By default, the program names the pictures using the name of the original document, followed by the image number of its position in the document. Press the x on the tab for the current image.

8. Click the **Yes** button on the display box to keep the name and the default location. Click **Save.**

9. Repeat with the other image to finish the exercise.

By selecting the Images option, the images that are in the PDF document you are using are numbered.

Imported images from a PDF document are individual documents in Photoshop and, as such, saved as any other Photoshop file.

Saving images as PDF

YOU CAN USE THE SAVE AS OPTION in the File menu, and, you can store RGB, Indexed, CMYK, Grayscale Bitmaps, Lab, and Duotones in the Portable Document Format (PDF). In addition, Photoshop also includes an automatic action in the Default Actions set in the Actions panel that performs this process automatically.

1. Use one of the open images that were used in these exercises, open the **File** menu and click **Save As**.

2. In the **Save As** box, click the button in the **Format** field, choose **Photoshop PDF** and click the **Save** button.

3. Press the **OK** button in the information box that appears.

4. In the **Save Adobe PDF** box, you should establish the save conditions for the document. You can use any of the presets that Photoshop offers or adjust the preferences as needed. Press the arrow button on the **Compatability** option and select **Acrobat 9/10 (PDF 1.7 +)**.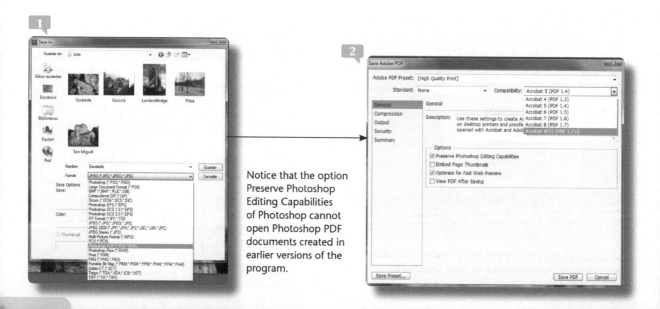

5. You can make adjustments to compression, output, and security, while in the **Summary** section, you can view the general

Notice that the option Preserve Photoshop Editing Capabilities of Photoshop cannot open Photoshop PDF documents created in earlier versions of the program.

settings. Click the check box of **View PDF After Saving** for the document to open in Acrobat after it has been saved in PDF format.

6. Press **Save Preset** to save the conditions you established.

7. As you can see, the settings for PDF are stored by default in the **Settings** folder of Photoshop, although you can change this location if desired. In the **Save** box **Name** field enter the term you want and press the **Save** button.

8. Click the **Save PDF** button to save the image.

9. A dialog box informs us that the **Preserve Photoshop Editing Capabilities** is not compatible with earlier versions of the program. Click the **Yes** button to continue.

10. As we already mentioned, in the Save options box, Photoshop automatically opens the image that has been converted into a PDF file, which can be shared with other users who don't have Photoshop. This file can be opened in Photoshop CS6 if you choose **Photoshop PDF** from the **Type** field in the **Open** box. To finish this exercise, close the PDF document by clicking on the x on the **Title Bar**.

IMPORTANT

Once the image is stored, it opens in Acrobat (logically you must have this application), so you can share with users who do not have Photoshop.

The settings for saving documents in PDF format are stored by default in the **Settings** folder of Photoshop with the extension.joboptions.

Creating panoramas with Photomerge

IMPORTANT

Photomerge technology offers different types of composition: automatic, in perspective, cylindrical, spherical, and collage. With the Spherical option you can produce stunning 360° panoramas.

○ Perspective

○ Cylindrical

○ Spherical

THE AUTOMIZE COMMAND CONTAINS the Photomerge option, which allows you to create a single panoramic picture from different originals. After selecting the images that will form the panorama, the program tries to create the composition automatically, referencing the colors and values of the documents. The composition may be of different types and, once created, can be saved in Photoshop format.

1. For this exercise you need two images that reflect a continuous landscape over two parts. You can use the sample files **095_1. jpg** and **095_2.jpg**, which are included in the download area of our website. You can begin conducting this process in two ways: first by opening the images you want to combine or by accessing the **Photomerge** box, from where you can select those files. Open the **File** menu, click on the **Automate** command and choose **Photomerge**.

2. If you had previously opened the original images in the Photoshop workspace and provided that they were in the same

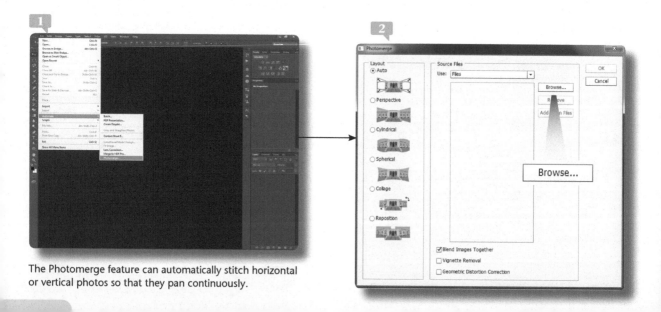

The Photomerge feature can automatically stitch horizontal or vertical photos so that they pan continuously.

095

order that they will appear in the composition, the log file names appear in the **Photomerge** box. Click on the **Browse** button. 2

3. In the **Open** dialog box, locate and select the first image of the composition and press the **Open** button.

4. Back in the **Photomerge** dialog box, press the **Browse** button and repeat the steps above to open the second image. 3

5. Note that the Photomerge Tool offers different modes of composition. If you keep the **Blend Images Together** options marked, the program will search for the best edges between images and their colors, and they will match perfectly. Keep the **Auto** layout mode and press **OK** to continue.

6. The program analyzes 4 the content of the two images to be joined and then merges them automatically so as to appear practically perfect in one continuous image. 5 The two images that form the panorama occupy two distinct layers to which Photoshop has automatically added the layer masks necessary for the perfect union. Thus should it ever need retouching, you can do each image separately. To save this composition in the Photoshop format, open the **File menu,** click on the **Save** option, and select the Photoshop format in the **Format** field and then press **Save.**

When you start the joining process, Photoshop analyzes the content of the images to properly align layers to create the panorama.

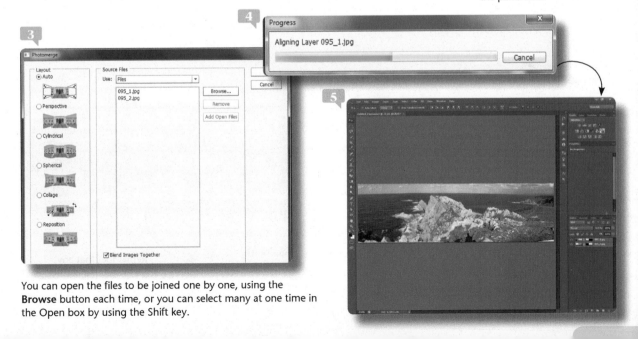

You can open the files to be joined one by one, using the **Browse** button each time, or you can select many at one time in the Open box by using the Shift key.

Creating panoramic compositions

THE AUTOMATIC PHOTOMERGE FEATURE allows you to create compositions in perspective, by designating one of the source images as a reference image; cylindrical, showing each of the images as if it were an open cylinder; spherical, aligning and transforming the image as if it were to be assigned within a sphere; in collage, aligning the layers by the overlapping content, and finally, aligning the layers to make sure that any overlapping content doesn't change (or stretch or skew) any of the layers.

1. In this exercise you will see some results that can be obtained through different modes of the panoramic Photomerge composition that are available to the user. You can use images **096_1.png, 096_2.png** and **096_3.png**, which are available on our website. Once opened in the Photoshop workspace, open the **Photomerge** box as you did in the previous exercise and, once there, click the **Add Open Files** button. 🔲

2. Begin with the type of composition called **Perspective**, which will achieve a consistent composition by designating one of the source images (by default, the central image) as the reference image. In the **Layout** section, check the **Perspective** op-

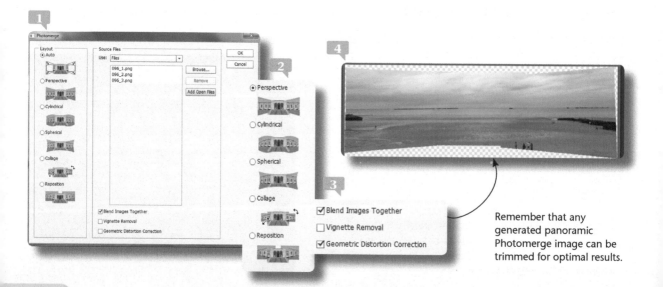

Remember that any generated panoramic Photomerge image can be trimmed for optimal results.

tion, 🔲 click on the **Geometric Distortion Correction** option to make the program purge any distortion errors 🔲 then press **OK** to check the effect.

3. Asides from the central image designated as a reference, the other two images are then transformed (repositioned, stretched or skewed as necessary) in a way so that any overlapping will be aligned. 🔲 The final image is good, but you would like to do better. Try another one of the compositions available in Photomerge. With image **096_1.png** in the foreground and from the **Photomerge** box, check the **Cylindrical** option and then press the OK button. 🔲

4. This type of cylindrical composition reduces distortion in the shape of a bow tie, which can be generated with the composition in perspective, because it shows each of the images as if it were an open cylinder. 🔲 In the cylindrical compositions, the reference image is at the center. This mode of composition is the ideal choice for creating wide panoramas. Let's look at a third type of image composition, called **Collage**, by which the program aligns matching layers with any overlapping content, while it transforms (rotates or scales) any of the original layers. With image **096_1.png** in the foreground, as you have previously accessed the **Photomerge** box and added the open files in the workspace, select the **Collage** option, then press the **OK** button to check the result. 🔲

Creating a 360° panorama

THE COMBINATION OF THE FUNCTIONS within Photomerge to create 3D shapes in Photoshop can create spectacular 360° panoramas or place them on a sphere. It is essential to photograph a complete circle of images with sufficient overlap. You will get better results by using a panoramic head on a tripod.

1. To complete this exercise, use the nine sample files in the folder **097**, which can be downloaded as usual from our website and saved on your computer. When available, access the **Photomerge** box, expand the **Use** field, click on the **Folder** option and use the **Browse** button to find the location and selection of the folder you need.

2. The images are neatly loaded in the **Photomerge** box. Now, you must choose the composition mode that is suitable for your purpose. In this case, click on the mode called **Spherical**, check the **Geometric Distortion Together** option and press the **OK** button to create the new landscape. 🔲

3. After the layers have rapidly been aligned, the new panorama appears in the workspace. 🔲 In the second part of this exercise

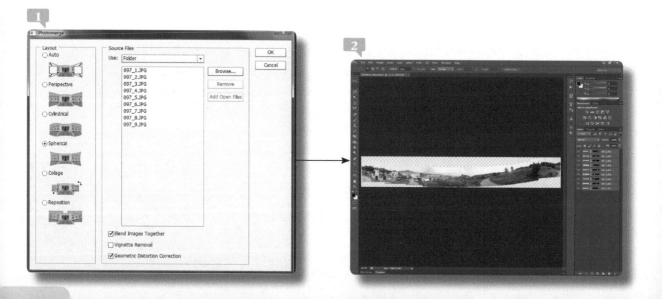

097

you will use the spherical panorama to move the new image onto a 3D sphere. To do this, display the **3D menu**, click the **New Mesh from Layer** command, click on the **Mesh Preset** option and choose from the list of available 3D shapes called **Spherical Panorama.**

4. Believe it or not, your goal has been achieved. To check, change the document display. In the window at the top left of the 3D scene, click on the icon showing an arrow and choose the option change to **Front** view.

5. Now, click on the icon at the top right of this window to switch to the secondary 3D view and to check the finished result.

6. Now, the work area shows a drawing of a ball wrapped in the panoramic image you created with Photomerge. To check the result in a better way, double-click on the zoom range of the **Status Bar**, then enter a value of 100 and press **Return.**

7. The areas that are white correspond to transparent pixels, which are generated in the panorama and can be hidden manually by placing the relevant upper and lower images, taken at the time. Should you not have these pictures, you can choose to paint the remaining transparent pixels in the 3D spherical panorama layer. Complete this exercise by saving the current image.

IMPORTANT

With the spherical mode, the program generates an image with several layers from the source images, adding layer masks as needed to create an optimal fusion where images overlap.

	Default
	Left
	Right
✓	Top
	Bottom
	Back
	Front
	Vanishing Point Grid
	Camera_1

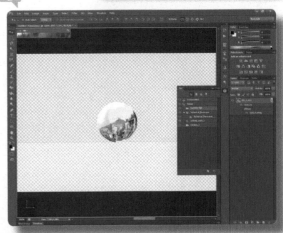

Creating thumbnails

THE CONTACT SHEET CREATES A SERIES OF thumbnail previews on a page that can then be printed. The thumbnails take the size you specify, such as, for example, the contact sheet. In addition, through the Contact Sheet II dialog box, you can distribute the thumbnails in the number of columns and rows you think necessary.

1. Use a folder that contains several of the images that you have worked with in these exercises. To begin, open the **File** menu, click the command **Automate** and choose **Contact Sheet II**.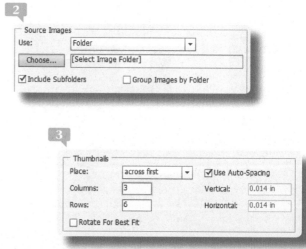

2. In the **Contact Sheet II** dialog box, specify the images you want to include on the contact sheet. Press the **Choose** button in the **Source Images** section.

3. In the **Choose a Folder** box, locate and select your folder and press **OK**.

4. Click the **Include Subfolders** check box.

5. Then specify the number of columns and rows you want for the thumbnails. In the **Thumbnails** section, enter a value of **3** in the **Columns** field.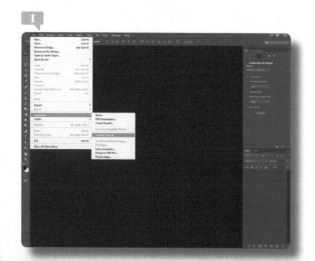

6. Keep the number of rows displayed by default. The **Use File-name as Caption** section that you find checked allows you to choose the option to place the file name under each image. You can assign a different font and size from the default one, as well as even disable this option. To complete the configuration, click **OK.**

7. After importing, which will take more or less time depending on the content of your folder, Photoshop will have automatically generated the thumbnail documents in your folder. Under each file, the name appears. If you have created more than one page, click on the tab of the first page.

8. Now you will fit the contact sheet to the screen. Click the **Zoom Tool** in the **Tools** pane and click the **Fit Screen** button to display the **Options Bar.**

9. To finish, you will save and close the contact sheets. Click the x button on the first sheet of contacts and in the box that appears, press the **Yes** button.

10. Keep the name and location shown by default in the **Save As** box, then click the **Save** button. Repeat with the other contact sheets if necessary.

IMPORTANTE

In order to create contact sheets in Photoshop CS6, the corresponding plug-in, which can be downloaded from the Adobe website, should be added. With this download, you will find a PDF document that will guide you through the installation of the plug-in for it to work properly.

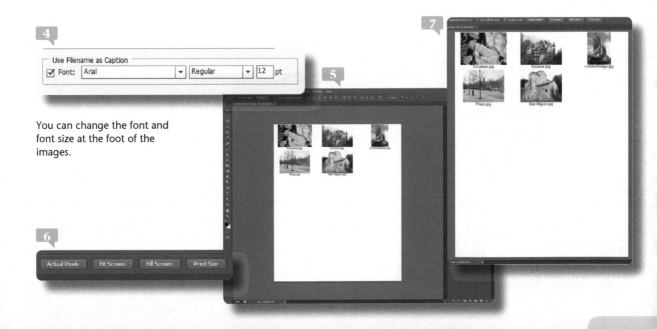

You can change the font and font size at the foot of the images.

Creating web photo galleries

TO AUTOMATICALLY CREATE a web page that contains a collection of images selected by the user, we use the Web Photo Gallery Automate command from the File menu. The Web Photo Gallery box offers several styles to create the page, which can be modified in various ways, such as the size of the images, the text and specifications about the author of the photographs or the creator.

1. To perform this exercise, you can reuse the folder of images you used in the previous exercise. Open the **File** menu, click the **Automate** command and choose **Web Photo Gallery**. 🔲

2. In the **Web Photo Gallery** dialog box, you will indicate how it will look as a website. Open the **Styles** menu box, click the bottom of the vertical scroll bar and select the style **simple-vertical thumbnails**. 🔲

3. In the **E-mail** field specify an email address so that users visiting the page can contact the photographer or the creator of the web page. Click the **Browse** button in the **Source Images** section, then locate and select your file in the **Search folder** and click **OK**.

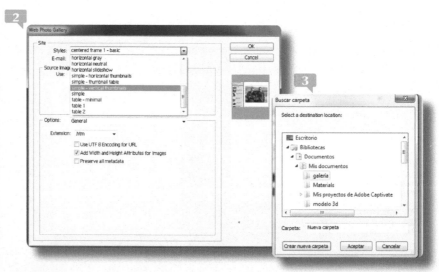

4. Next, specify the destination for the files that Photoshop automatically creates, so that the web page can be displayed without any problems. Press the **Destination** button of this subsection, and again in the **Search folder,** locate and select the desired directory then click **OK.**

5. In the options section you can modify a large number of properties of the gallery that you are going to create, such as the size of the images and their thumbnails, the security level by adding copyright, etc. Click the arrow button in the **Options** field and choose the **Banner** option.

6. You can add all the information that you feel is important, for example, concerning the photographer's name, contact details, and date of creation of the gallery. Open the menu of the **Options** field and choose **Custom Colors.**

7. In this section, you can select the background color of the page, the text, the text links, and the text links already visited, depending on the style chosen. Customize the page to your liking and when finished, click **OK** to create the page.

IMPORTANT

In order to create web photo galleries in Photoshop CS6, you should add the corresponding plug-in, which can be downloaded from the Adobe website. When you download this plug-in, you will find a PDF document that will guide you through the correct installation of the plug-in so that it works properly.

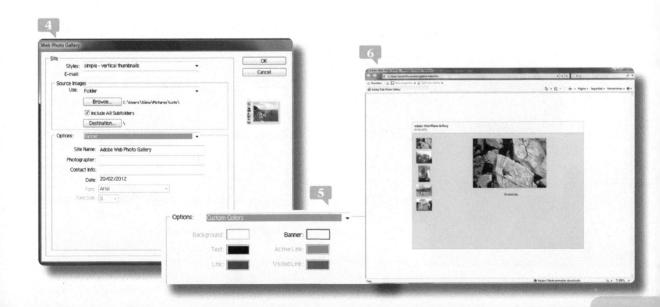

Working with groups of images

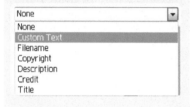

THE PICTURE PACKAGE COMMAND ALLOWS YOU to include several copies of an image on one page. To do this, you must access the dialog box with the same name, select the image you want to include, and determine the number of times you want to duplicate it, its orientation, and the resolution. You can duplicate the same image up to 20 times.

1. Open the **File** menu, click the **Automate** command and select **Picture Package.** 🔲

2. The **Picture Package** dialog box appears with options to select the origin of the group of images to import, the imported document features, and commands to implement some actions. First, select the source image. Click on the arrow button of the **Use** field and choose the **Folder** option. 🔲

3. To locate the folder containing the images you want to import, click the **Browse** button.

4. In the **Search folder**, locate and select your sample folder and click **OK.** 🔲

5. After selecting the set of source images, you can modify some of the properties of each of them. In the **Document** section,

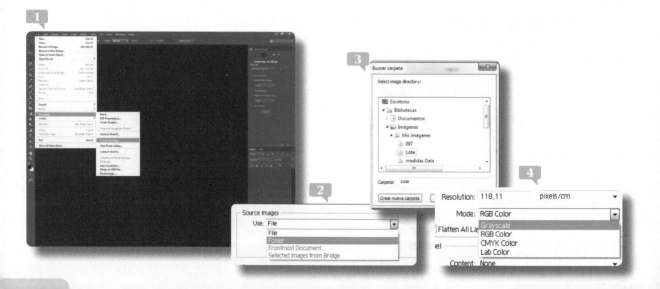

you can set the page size, the composition, the resolution, and the color mode. By default, the **Layout** field displays the format (2) 5x7, indicating that the imported image will appear doubled. Open the **Mode** list box and choose **Grayscale.**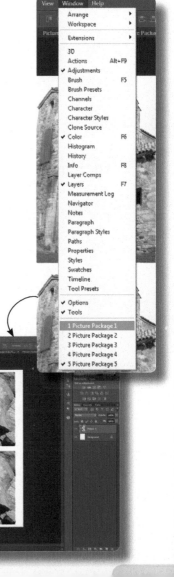

6. Then, you will include customized text on the document. In the **Label** section, open the **Content** list and choose **Custom Text.**

7. Click the **Custom Text** field and type in a title.

8. Keep the font and size, although you will modify the color. Pull down the **Color** list box and choose **White** to highlight text on images.

9. You can also choose the position of the text on the image, which by default is set to focus and in this case, you will keep this as it is. Click **OK**.

10. The process, whose duration depends on the number of imported images, is complete: the images are loaded into the workspace with the settings defined. Pull down the **Window** menu and click on **Picture Package 1.**

11. As you can see from the **Window** menu, you have successfully created the sets of images contained in your folder. Finish this exercise by closing it without saving the changes. Open the **File** menu, click the **Close All** option and press the **No** button in the following dialog boxes so that the changes are not saved.

To continue learning...

IF THIS BOOK HAS FULFILLED YOUR EXPECTATIONS

This book is part of a collection that covers the most commonly used and known software in all professional areas.

All the books in the collection share the same aproach as the one you have just finished. So, if you would like to know more about other software packages, on the next page, you will find other books in this collection.

OPERATING SYSTEMS

If you are interested in operating systems, then *'Learning Windows 8 with 100 practical exercises'* is, without a doubt, the book that you are looking for.

Microsoft is launching a new version of its Windows operating system, which is full of new additions that are both visual and functional. The biggest change is seen as soon as you open the program: you are presented with a new personalized screen, giving you direct access to the Metro programs and applications, which you can set up on your PC and anywhere you can access your PC (such as the cloud). The new Metro interface has been designed for touch screen devices.

With this book:

- You will practice with the Windows Explorer Ribbon.
- You will work with the renewed and advanced Task Manager.
- You will use the new security and maintenance tools so that your PC will always be as protected as much as possible.

CREATING AND EDITING WEB SITES

If you are interested in creating and editing personal or professional websites, then *'Learning Dreamweaver CS6 with 100 practical exercises'* is perfect for you.

Dreamweaver is the industry standard for creating and editing web pages. This is the ideal software for web designers and developers to graphic designers. With this manual you will learn how to use it easily and conveniently.

With this book:

- You will meet the new grid-based CSS layout and work more comfortably with multiscreen options than before.
- You will make transitions based on CSS3 to apply smooth changes in the properties of the elements of a page.
- You will use creative web sources compatible with the Internet in Dreamweaver.
- You will apply the same elements in multiple CSS classes.

COLLECTION LEARNING... WITH 100 PRACTICAL EXERCISES

IN PREPARATION...

DESIGN AND ASSISTED CREATIVITY

- Dreamweaver CS6
- Flash CS6
- Illustrator CS6
- Photographical Retouch with Photoshop CS6

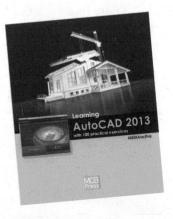